A Phantom Stallion's Wild Ride

...I could hear the horse racing toward us down the narrow country road. Its metal shoes clanged against the road and echoed from the steep hillsides like rolling thunder.

I pulled Crystal, my five-year-old daughter, to safety behind a large tree so the horse would not trample us as it passed. "The rider must be crazy to ride that fast down a narrow crooked road like this," I thought. "Someone could get killed if he doesn't slow that beast down.

"The pounding hooves were almost upon us. I peered cautiously around the tree and waited for the animal to come around the bend in the road. It never did...

Excerpt from "The Ghost of Crazy Horse Hollow," on page 174.

Phantom Army of the Civil War

and other Southern Ghost Stories

Compiled and Edited by
Frank Spaeth

From the Files of **FATE** Magazine

CASTLE BOOKS

This edition published in 2000 by Castle Books,
a division of Book Sales, Inc.
114 Northfield Avenue
Edison, NJ 08837

Reprinted by agreement and permission of
Llewellyn Publications
P.O. Box 64383
St. Paul, MN 55164

Cataloging-in-Publication Data:

Phantom army of the Civil War: and other southern ghost
    stories/compiled and edited by Frank Spaeth from the files of
    Fate Magazine. – 1st ed.
    p. cm. – "The stories were selected from articles previously
published in Fate Magazine." – Introd.
    1. Ghosts – Southern States. 2. Ghost Stories, American –
Southern States. 3. Haunted houses – Southern States. I. Spaeth,
Frank, 1971-. II. Fate (Chicago, Ill.)
    BF1472.U6P43   1997
    133.1'0975 --- dc21   97-9237
                                                 CIP

ISBN 0-7858-1287-3

Table of Contents

Introduction

I remember once as a child, four or five years old, waking up in the middle of the night and peering out from my bed into the hallway. I had been drawn to look in that direction by unfamiliar movement and light. It was as if a circle of illuminated beings were dancing in a circle. I remember watching with both interest and confusion at the strange sight. I'll probably never know what was dancing there—whether it was a ghostly manifestation or simply a dream—but I do know that the event is forever etched in my memory.

Few stories are as intriguing as a good ghostly tale. When the stories of menacing phantoms and haunted houses have a basis in fact, it can add quite a hair-raising effect to that basic intrigue. For nearly 50 years FATE Magazine has informed and entertained readers with stories of ghosts, UFOs, and other unexplained phenomena. One of my favorite editorial tasks is reading the wonderful, strange, sometimes scary stories of people's experiences with the unknown, especially those dealing with ghosts. Reading so many ghost tales can certainly cause one to wonder what, or who, is causing such disturbances...and why?

This book is filled with stories relating personal encounters with spirits throughout the South, filled with a flavor and tone that is truly and uniquely Southern. The stories were selected from articles previously published in FATE Magazine. They cover a span of over forty years, and represent the best Southern ghost stories ever to appear in FATE, the world's oldest magazine featuring true reports of the strange and unknown.

These ghosts come in various shapes and sizes—men, women, children, and even animals. People involved with these stories report having seen, heard, and sometimes even smelled an apparition in their proximity. Stories come from professional paranormal investigators and from average people—you don't have to be an expert in the field of ghosts to encounter one!

Some of the ghosts featured are angry and confused, looking for answers as to why they are no longer among the living. Other spirits seem to have stayed around to guide and protect loved ones. There are even ghosts that don't seem to notice those living around them. That's one of the crazy things about ghosts. Like most supernatural encounters, no two haunting experiences seem to be alike.

The rich and emotional history of the South adds something extra special to this compilation. Some of these spirits lived, fought, and died during the Civil War, our country's bloodiest, costliest conflict. Others were around long before that, helping to fight for independence from the British. Still others fought to tame the wild lands as the nation expanded West.

Not every ghost story presented here deals with wars or battles. There are other fascinating tales of phantom grandmothers looking after and protecting their grandchildren from beyond the grave. There are stories of lost love and betrayed love—phantoms who roam the countryside searching for a love they cannot find. Every story is different and unique, offering something for everyone—whether you believe in ghosts of not.

The chapters of this compilation are presented alphabetically by state, but some of you may not find a story from your state. Don't worry! It isn't because your state isn't Southern enough or because it has no ghosts. We simply did not have enough ghost stories from your state to fill a chapter. If your state is not mentioned, and you have a true ghost account to share, send it to me and we'll consider it for a second book or for FATE magazine.

I hope you enjoy reading this compilation as much as I enjoyed putting it together. These stories are only a few of the hundreds of ghostly tales that have been printed in the pages of FATE—stories from the South, as well as the rest of the country and the rest of the world.

—Frank Spaeth
Associate Editor
FATE Magazine

Phantom Army of the Civil War

By Frank Spaeth

December 1996

The heavy emotions of battle can linger long after combatants have finished their duty. Many Civil War battlefields are said to be sites of ghostly reenactments of the United States' most deadly conflict. But there is one battle that is fought elsewhere—in the hallway of a famous General's house.

It's the middle of the night. The air is filled with the sounds of battle—the roar of cannons and the screams of soldiers. The shadows of phantoms in blue and grey lurk in every corner. War rages all around. It isn't just any war, but the Civil War—the most costly war in terms of lost lives—and lost innocence—in United States history.

Many Civil War battlefields are rife with stories and legends of ghostly soldiers and phantom armies, but there is one Civil War battle that isn't relived on the battlefield. Instead, the horrors of war come to life in the New Orleans mansion of a famous Confederate general.

The Beauregard-Keyes house, located in the French Quarter of New Orleans, has a long, colorful history. Built in the 1820s, the mansion has been home to many famous people, including novelist Francis Parkinson Keyes. The ghostly rumors, however, surround another important figure.

General Pierre Gustave Toutant Beauregard moved into the mansion shortly after the Civil War ended, although he may have resided there with his family during the war as well. Forced by illness to retire, Beauregard, a member of a prominent family in the New Orleans area, came home. He had graduated from West Point in 1838 and fought in the Mexican War. He was in command of the Confederate forces that fired on Fort Sumter in April 1861. A year later he led his troops at the Battle of Shiloh.

Shiloh was one of the most brutal battles of the Civil War. Over 23,000 men—10,000 Confederate troops and 13,000 Union soldiers—lost their lives in two days of intense fighting. Although the Union was the technical victor, the Battle of Shiloh was important to the Confederacy as well, for it stabilized their western position. In any case, the emotional scars of the battle were forever etched on every soldier who lived through—and died in—the Battle of Shiloh.

Nowhere may the eternal remembrance of Shiloh be more apparent than in the Beauregard-Keyes house. By day this beautifully restored Southern mansion, which has been designated a National Historic Place, is a thriving inn. Guides in period costume entertain guests, showing them the house's intricacies. But late at night, those wandering around may be greeted by another, less pleasing spectacle.

Over the years, stories of a ghostly battle reenactment have circulated. According to reports some nights at approximately 2:00 A.M. strange events take place in and around the mansion's ballroom. The area takes on an otherworldly feel. The lavish furnishings seem to fade away, replaced by wide open spaces—battle grounds—and the hearty spirits of Beauregard's troops at the Battle of Shiloh. General Beauregard enters the battle from the ballroom's large double doors, riding his great white steed.

Legions of men under his command struggle against other spectral forces. Eventually the Confederate phantoms begin to show the wear of battle. The seemingly healthy ghosts change. Well-conditioned limbs become broken, mangled, and useless. Soldier's faces are wiped away, leaving fleshless skulls with hollow eye sockets. The stench of rotting death fills the hallway. Men groan in agony and cry for help. But even in death, the men can't escape their fates. Then suddenly, the light of day comes and silence falls over the area. The soldiers fade away. Their eternal battle will continue some other night.

Psychically sensitive people have been overwhelmed by feelings of anguish, confusion, and despair while visiting the hallway and ballroom of the Beauregard-Keyes house—emotions which most witnesses feel resonate from its spectral soldiers.

Psychic Luann Wolfe, who has visited the site of the actual Battle of Shiloh, in Tennessee, says that these kinds of feelings are common in places where a tremendous loss of life has occurred. She felt the horror emanating from the Shiloh battlefield and has received similar readings at other battlefield sites, as well.

Although many visitors claim to have witnessed this incredible ghostly battle, there is one woman who questions the authenticity of the stories. Marion Chambon is the director of the Beauregard-Keyes house. She says that she does not know of anyone who has personally experienced the return of Beauregard's army. But she adds, "This is a very old house and it can get a little creepy, not scary, at times. In the winter when it gets dark early, the house—or something—can sometimes 'spook' me, and for no reason I lock up very quickly and leave."

Mrs. Chambon went on to explain, "If we do have ghosts or spirits here then they are happy ones, and they leave us alone and we leave them alone."

Mrs. Chambon is skeptical about the phantom army, but she has an open mind toward the possibility of other ghostly happenings around the house. She cites a book entitled *The Beauregard-Keyes House*, by Samuel Wilson, Jr., which shares another ghostly tale.

Apparently, General Beauregard and his wife had planned a grand ball in the house. Unfortunately, the General was called away on business and the ball never took place. It is said that every once in a while the ghosts of the Beauregards return to the ballroom to host the ball they planned but never gave.

Chambon relates a story that adds some credibility to the phantom ball tale. A young girl rented out the apartment below the ballroom one night. According to Chambon, the next morning, when the girl was asked how her night was, "She stated that she did not get much sleep that night because of the music and sounds of furniture being moved."

Was it the sound of long-deceased reveling debutantes coming to the ball that never took place? Or was it the sound of the hallway transforming into a battleground for ghostly soldiers? No one can say for sure, but many people have left the Beauregard-Keyes house feeling that there is more inside than the simple furnishings of a renovated Civil War mansion.

ALABAMA

If Ghosts Could Kill...

By Glen I. Taylor

April 1989

Spook was no good-natured haunt—his stunts seemed designed to expose victims to deadly danger.

Smith Lake in northern Alabama occupies a large portion of Cullman, Walker, and Winston counties. The lake was developed by the Alabama Power Company in the 1950s to generate electricity for northern Alabama. After completion of the lake about 1960, the power company stocked it with game fish in order to attract sportsmen, and started selling waterfront property. The lake consists of some 500 miles of shoreline in the middle of beautiful timber country, a perfect setting for anybody's fishing cabin.

My half-sister Katie and her husband Lonnie purchased a lot near Big Bridge Marina in the early '60s and started building a two-story cabin. For Katie, who was in her mid-30's, and Lonnie, about 40, the cabin became an every weekend retreat. Both liked fishing, and not having any children, they were free to do pretty much as they pleased. Only one floor of the cabin was erected at this time, with plans to complete the upper level in the near future.

When they were not fishing, Katie worked around the cabin planting flowers and shrubbery. Katie had always loved pretty flowers, as much as Lonnie loved fishing, which he could do day and night. Before long the lakeside cottage began to look like a miniature Cypress Gardens, which Katie used to visit occasionally.

Soon Katie found herself spending more time alone at the cabin with her beautification project and less time fishing with Lonnie. It was then she noticed strange things going on around the place. Sometimes while she was working on her flower beds with no one around, someone or something would touch her. The touchings weren't regular or predictable, but they were frequent and they drove Katie crazy. She'd be touched on the neck, arm, or leg and she couldn't figure out what was causing it.

Katie did not believe in ghosts and had always been a fairly level-headed person. Nevertheless, the touching incidents continued. For some reason Katie was the only person who experienced the phenomena.

I remember when I was about nine years old, she would talk about things touching her, and Lonnie would laugh, saying her imagination was playing tricks on her because she spent too much time in the cabin alone. He told her to pay no attention to it. This was easy advice for Lonnie, but Katie was becoming unnerved by the strangeness of the whole thing and wasn't willing to believe her mind was playing tricks on her.

It was about then that Katie saw the stranger for the first time. She was in bed when Lonnie left the cabin about four in the morning so he could be fishing at daybreak. Katie woke from a sound sleep to find someone standing at the foot of her bed. She could see his figure illuminated by the pale light coming through a bay window.

He wore a black cloak and hat such as the Puritans wear in pictures. He had a narrow face, a sharp chin, and deep-set dark eyes. Katie rolled over in bed to look at the figure again, but he was gone.

This incident really gave her the creeps. She couldn't understand why the man would be standing over the bed watching her sleep.

She later told the story of her strange visitor to Lonnie and other family members. They responded with loud laughter and remarks about having her put away. Naturally they were joking, but I had never seen a ghost and had never been touched unexplainably either, so the stories Katie told made me laugh along with everyone else.

After the incident with the stranger, Katie began to dread being in the cabin alone, so she started keeping someone with her. I have a nephew, Terry, by a half-sister. Terry and I are the same age and we became regular visitors to the cabin. It was a fair trade-off. Terry and I went fishing and swimming and acted as Katie's bodyguards when needed. During the day it didn't matter where we went or what we did, but come nightfall we had to be there with her to keep the ghost away, so she said.

Before long the second floor of the cabin was completed and we made the transition upstairs. Even after the move upstairs, strange things continued to happen. Once, when I was about 12 years old, I was sleeping in the living room on a fold-out sofa. At that age, and with all the reports of weird events, I was afraid to stay in the back bedroom alone.

Katie was awakened that morning by the cover on her bed being pulled off her from the foot end. Since Katie knew she and I were the only people in the cabin, she thought I was playing a trick on her. When the cover was almost pulled off the bed, she grabbed it and called out my name. When I didn't answer, she sat up in bed to see who was pulling the cover. No one was there. From where she was sitting on the bed, she had a view of the living room and saw that I was still asleep on the sofa.

The touching continued with the move to the upper floor of the cabin. One morning in the same room where the cover-pulling incident took place, Katie was sleeping without covers and awoke to the sensation that someone was rubbing her leg.

Katie, being honest as she is, continued to tell us about the little encounters as they occurred. As it was, no one but Katie had been touched or seen anything unusual, so it was getting hard to believe her stories without some real evidence to support them.

I remember that once Katie woke up in the middle of the night and saw a woman dressed in a pink negligee standing in the doorway which separated the hall and living room. The lady had yellow-blond hair and stood about five feet, six inches tall, as Katie recalled, but the description didn't fit anyone in the cabin at that particular time. Unfortunately, no one but Katie saw the blond lady. As usual it was always Katie who saw these strange visitors as if they were trying to remain invisible to everyone else.

Even with the strange happenings going on, nobody seemed to be in any real danger, and sometimes Katie would even laugh when telling her stories. Unfortunately, the phenomena didn't stay harmless.

A set of steps separated the upper yard from the lower, which had a chain link fence around it. One day Katie was working around the cabin and started walking down the steps to the lower yard. As she explained it, about halfway down something grabbed her ankle. As she struggled to free herself, she fell all the way to the bottom of the steps and sustained a broken leg. Fortunately another adult was there besides us kids, so she was immediately taken to the hospital and a cast was put on her leg from the knee down.

As time went on it became more evident that something was present in and around the cabin, and that Katie's mind was not playing tricks on her. Another sister of mine, Sara, had a frightening experience with Katie's ghost friend in the basement of the cabin. Sara, her husband Billy, and Katie were going up the stairs when something grabbed Sara's ankle. She knew Billy was behind her, so she stopped and demanded, "Billy, let go of my leg!"

Billy replied, "I'm not holding your leg." As she looked around, her ankle was released and she saw Billy standing where he couldn't have reached her. She realized that whatever had grabbed her leg, it wasn't Billy and she was horrified at the thought that the ghost may have threatened her. Sara, about 40 at the time, became the second person to have direct contact with the strange presence, to which we started referring as "Spook." After Sara's experience the touching stopped and the cabin remained quiet for a long time.

A few years later, Katie was planting flowers on a hillside in front of the cabin. Terry was helping her as he often did. Suddenly she fell. This time she sustained a broken arm and said that she was pushed by someone, although no one had been seen. She was taken to the hospital again and a cast was put on her arm.

The strange happenings continued throughout the years, but it wasn't until I was 16 that I had an encounter with Spook.

One fall evening Katie and I were watching television in the living room. We were alone in the cabin that night, Lonnie was fishing, and Katie wanted me to stay with her since it was late. In the middle of the program I got up to fix a snack and when I returned to my seat, Katie turned to me and said, "Glen, you left that cabinet door open." I looked into the kitchen and sure enough, the cabinet door was standing wide open.

I replied, "I'll close it when I finish eating," and we continued watching the movie. A couple of minutes later we heard a loud noise in the kitchen. We turned around in our chairs and saw that the cabinet door was shut. Some-one, Spook apparently, had slammed the door. It was cold outside so all of the doors and windows in the cabin were closed. Therefore, the cupboard door could not have been shut by a draft.

Katie and I looked at each other. Katie said, "See what I mean, I guess now you'll believe me!"—which was the understatement of the year. At that time I truly began to believe, no doubt about it. I sat in my chair with chill bumps all over my body.

When Lonnie came in from fishing we told him about the cabinet door closing by itself, but as usual he just laughed. I became the third person to have personal contact with Spook, and another one to be laughed at, along with Katie and Sara.

About a year later, in October 1974, a man who lived in the cabin next to ours was missing for four days. Lonnie and I found him floating in the lake under his boat dock. The death was ruled accidental by the authorities since there was no evidence of foul play. The man had been fishing on the night of the accident. When his sister returned to join him at the cabin, she found the door open and all the lights on in the cabin and boathouse.

There was no real evidence that Spook had anything to do with the man's death. But the police officer's theory of what he suspected had happened made me think of Spook. The officer said the man had apparently tripped or caught his foot on something and fallen into the lake. From what I could see there was nothing on the pier over which the man could have tripped or caught his foot on.

But I thought of Katie's broken leg and arm, of Sara's ankles being grabbed on the basement stairs, and the cabinet door closing by itself. The man could have been tripped but I don't believe it was by an object. The dead man had been about 45 years old and his sister said he was a good swimmer. The shoreline was only a few feet away from the pier. I have my suspicions as to why the man couldn't swim to safety.

Shortly after the man's death I enlisted in the Army and moved away. I had no more encounters with Spook after that, but occasionally when I hear someone say, "Ghosts can't hurt you, they only make you hurt yourself," I am inclined to tell them about Spook and the man who died when he tripped over something that wasn't there.

The Ghost Who Graduated

By Mai Kampitt

April 1969

His life nipped in the bud, a boy's concern for his career and companions survived as a potent, punctual force.

I never knew Douglas Williams, for my tenure as an instructor at Blount High School in Prichard, Alabama, began with the 1957-1958 school year. I am told he was a happy-go-lucky but studious young man. He enjoyed school both for studies and sports and he excelled in everything he did.

Just as enthusiastically Doug engaged in the whirl-wind of summer activities with his schoolmates—boating, beach parties, water skiing, softball—and he also had a paper route. Summer vacation was nearing its close when one sultry August afternoon he was cycling along Main Street on his way to deliver the evening papers.

Perhaps his mind was wandering—as a boy's will—but he recognized Mrs. Randall, a family acquaintance, standing at a bus stop. She waved to him and as he raised one hand to return the greeting she saw the car he didn't see. The vehicle slammed into him, the driver speeding away. It happened so quickly that later Mrs. Randall remembered nothing of the car, nothing but the sight of Doug's shattered bike and his crumpled body lying broken and dying in a welter of the scattered evening papers.

September came and with it my first job as a teacher. I was fresh out of college and very pleased to have an excellent position in a large high school in my own hometown.

My classes, five in all, were composed of eleventh and twelfth grade Business English and Business Law students and I had a homeroom of seniors. Soon everything was in full swing and I learned about Douglas Williams.

His classmates, football teammates, and coaches talked about him a lot. He had been an outstanding player, I gathered. The principal and coaches organized a brief memorial service and authorized that his jersey, number 22, be retired. Ceremoniously and with reverence they placed it in the school's trophy case.

I learned, too, that Doug had planned to have his own business after finishing college and the previous year had been assigned to what was now my homeroom, students majoring in Business. The schedule had not changed from last year and they were scheduled to come to me for Business English from 11:00 to 12:00 o'clock each day.

Before many weeks had passed one of my students, Jane Bennett, noticed something puzzling occurring each day. To be sure she was not mistaken she waited a week or so before calling it to my attention.

When she did mention it she told me that each day at precisely 11:20 the door to the classroom slowly opened. It had opened frequently since the class was assigned to me but each time I merely said, without so much as lifting my eyes, "Will someone close the door, please?" Now the matter lay open for discussion, for Jane had jotted down the exact time the door opened each day.

"I'm certain it's nothing more than the wind—a draft, perhaps—that causes the door to open," I said. "I'll ask the janitor to check the latch and the hinges this afternoon.'

The janitor found one hinge that needed tightening and he did this while I stood watching him. I shared this information with my class the next day when it convened at 11:00 A.M. and considered the matter closed.

For 20 minutes that morning it remained closed. But at precisely 11:20, as it had done on previous mornings, the door quietly opened!

"It's Doug!" I heard someone whisper.

"What's that?" I asked, a little sharply.

Timidly one of the girls began to speak, expressing what the rest of the students undoubtedly thought too.

"Doug would have graduated with the rest of us but—" Her voice broke but she went on. "All of his classes were to have been with us, those of us in this room. I—we think he's the one who opens the door every day."

"Nonsense," I admonished, as gently as I could. "There's a logical explanation for this and eventually we'll find it." I coaxed them to stop thinking about it and get back to their studies but deep down I began to wonder...for every day at 11:20, whether the day was rainy, cold, windy, calm, or sunny, the door opened. When this happened the class members inevitably looked at each other commiseratingly. Then someone would rise quietly and close it. The door never opened of itself again after 11:20 had passed.

The following June, 1958, the class graduated. In the 10 years since, no other class in that particular room has had the experience we now relive so vividly in our memories. In some way beyond our power of knowing, did Doug manage after all to graduate with his class?

The Uneasy Dead at Fort Mims

by Sally Remaley

December 1968

Perhps the spirits of the long departed are trying to tell the truth about what really happened at Fort Mims...and why.

After a century and a half, war whoops shatter the still night near the old fort. Would spirits rest in peace if the truth of the bloody massacre were known?

Floyd Boone, a young Bradenton, Florida, family man, graduate of the University of Alabama and state parole board employee, is probably one of the most logical and objective persons you could find. Yet a strange event, for which he can think of no logical or objective explanation, still bothers him after two years.

On March 27, 1966, Boone, who is descended on his mother's side from Chief Red Eagle, the famous Creek Indian leader, and on his father's side from Daniel Boone, American pioneer, took a friend, a man employed as a county probation supervisor in Florida, and journeyed to his home in Baldwin County, Alabama, to visit relatives in the little settlement where his father and a few remaining Creeks still live.

Boone is collecting historical data about his ancestors. Hoping to add to his material and information, he and his companion visited the site of the Massacre of Fort Mims. Because it was getting dark as they arrived, they decided to camp overnight on the grounds and further study the place the next day. The night was calm and still, with no wind. The two men curled up in their sleeping bags about 10:30 P.M. in the center of the barbed wire enclosure which now surrounds the site of old Fort Mims.

Back in 1813 news of the Massacre at Fort Mims spread across a shocked and saddened nation. A total of 516 men, women, and children were killed on August 30 that year by the Indians in one of the bloodiest slaughters ever recorded in American history. Today the event is almost forgotten. It even is unheard of by many persons living in this country today.

But Floyd Boone, who moved to Florida from his native Alabama in 1951, is a direct descendant of the famous Creek chief who at high noon on that day 155 years ago, led the attack on Fort Mims, Alabama, and he knows the story well. He has heard the tale since he was a little boy...from his father, his grandfather, and other members of his family.

The Massacre at Fort Mims, in Baldwin County, took place one month after the Battle of Burnt Corn, which was fought some 50 miles northeast of Tensaw in the same county. Both sites are approximately 35 miles north of Mobile, Alabama. The Burnt Corn battle was fought between the militia under the command of Colonel James Caller and the Creek Indians, then a powerful and proud nation. This battle, one in the historical conflict involving Spain, France, Great Britain, and the United States, ended in an embarrassing and disastrous defeat for the Americans. As a result the entire region of Alabama and surrounding areas were fearful.

Terrified settlers began moving into nearby forts and stockades, preparing to defend themselves. One such was Fort Mims which consisted of a stockade constructed around Samuel Mims's home, a large one-story frame structure with additional sheds, on land adjacent to Lake Tensaw.

Tension grew daily. Sentries kept a sharp lookout.

On August 29 two men, sent outside to herd cattle, rushed panic-stricken back to the safety of the fort crying, "Indians!" They reported seeing an unknown number of Indians wearing war paint.

The command at the fort immediately sent out a detachment of horsemen but these men found no trace of Indians.

The next day, August 30, a thousand Creek Indians, led by Chief Red Eagle whose American name was William (Billy) Weatherford, hid in a deep ravine just 400 yards east of the main gate at Fort Mims. As the signal of the dinner call sounded on a drum in the fort at high noon, the Creeks rushed across the open area surrounding the stockade, entered the east gate before those inside could close it and in four hours slaughtered everyone inside the fort with the exception of a few who escaped.

After the massacre soldiers from other forts in the region came to bury the dead. Not much remained of what had been Fort Mims and the healing touch of nature and the surrounding forest soon softened, then covered the hundreds of graves with a blanket of foliage.

General Andrew Jackson and his troops arrived at Fort Montgomery, not far from where Fort Mims had stood, and began the war to the finish with Chief Red Eagle and the Creeks. Skirmish after skirmish followed as more and more men joined the troops pledged to wipe out the Indians.

Only when the Creeks were almost all dead did the famous Indian chief, to save his nation from extinction, bow his proud head and surrender. History records the text of General William Weatherford's (Chief Red Eagle's) document of surrender which he wrote beautifully by hand, since he was a well-educated man. He delivered this orally to General Andrew Jackson at Tohopeka, Alabama, on the Tallapoosa River when he surrendered on March 28, 1814, eight months after the Massacre at Fort Mims.

This surrender message read in part: "I am in your power; do me as you please. I am a soldier, I have done the white people all the harm I could. I have fought them and fought them bravely. If I had an army I would yet fight...but...my people are all gone. I can do no more than to weep over the misfortunes of my nation.

"Once I could animate my warriors to battle but I cannot animate the dead. My warriors can no longer hear my voice. Their bones are at Talladega, Emunck-fow and Tohopeka....

"On the miseries and misfortunes brought upon my country I look back with deepest sorrow and wish to avert still greater calamities....

"You are a brave man and I rely on your generosity. You will exact no terms of conquered people but such as they can accede to.

"You have told us where we might go and be safe. This is good talk and my nation ought to listen to it. They shall listen to it. I shall say no more."

Now, on March 27, 1966, Floyd Boone, camping out on the site of old Fort Mims with his friend, could not sleep.

"It was chilly and we built a fire to keep warm," Boone said. "Shortly after settling down, we began to hear unusual noises. They sounded like moans...soft...but like something human. I raised up but saw nothing. I had lain back down trying to tell myself I had imagined it when my buddy suddenly jumped up and looked around. He said he thought he heard footsteps close by us but there was no one there. By this time we were both wide awake and decided the best thing to do was to stay awake and keep the fire going.

"Around 1:00 A.M., over the east gate of the fort, or where the east gate had been, we heard six loud drumbeats in succession. This was the entrance where Chief Red Eagle and his warriors entered the fort on the day of the massacre."

These drumbeats did not end the strange noises. In fact, the men said, they increased after that. Floyd's companion heard the sounds of horses' hooves, cries of human agony, muffled thuds, the sound of running feet, all the wild outcry of battle. And 2:00 A.M. two loud drumbeats sounded over the west gate area.

But Floyd and his buddy stuck it out.

"I kept telling myself it had to be my imagination," Floyd said."I never believed in ghosts."

Floyd's friend tried to tell himself the same thing even while he was actually hearing Indian war whoops, women screaming, men yelling, sounds so real it seemed to him the massacre was taking place all around him.

Still the two men could see nothing except the dark shadows of the lonely trees at the outer edge of the clearing and the moonlight shining across the field where the old fort once had stood. Not even a wild animal moved in the night, although the wild woodsy area must have been full of game, the men said. "At 4:00 A.M. we heard one drumbeat near where the blockhouse had stood," Floyd told me. "And that ended the strange incident. We heard no more unusual noises during the rest of the night but we sure were glad when morning came, believe me."

The two men think now that sleeping in the acre-square area where 516 bodies were buried in trenches by General Andrew Jackson and his troops isn't exactly the most inviting idea in the world.

"I don't know if I'd want to try it again or not," Boone confessed. "I wasn't really afraid. I was in familiar territory...I was born and raised in Alabama...but...."

Some persons who live in the area of the old fort and are familiar with its history suggest that perhaps the departed spirits of Chief Red Eagle, who led the attack on Fort Mims, and Major Daniel Beasley, who was commander of the fort at the time of the massacre, still are restless, still are wanting folks to know more about what happened and why on that long-ago day in August 1813.

History tells us that Major Daniel Beasley commanded the fort. General Claiborne, in command at Mount Vernon, came to Fort Mims August 7 to inspect this stockade and instructed Major Beasley "to strengthen the pickets and to build one or two additional blockhouses." Lieutenant William R. Chambliss stated after the attack, "And I further certify that Major Beasley received a letter, one or two days before the attack on Fort Mims, from General Claiborne (who was on his way to Fort Easley) advising him of the reported movements of the enemy." Major Beasley ignored all warnings, calling them false, and sent two notes to General Claiborne assuring him of his "ability to maintain the fort against any number of Indians."

Weatherford (Red Eagle) later explained to General Jackson and Thomas Woodward why he chose to stay with the Creeks. He said he realized there was no chance for the Indians to defeat the whites but he felt it was his duty to stay with them, to try to keep the tribe from being utterly destroyed. He was drawn into the Fort Mims expedition but did everything possible to warn the garrison there of the intended attack and felt that he would have succeeded had the commander, Beasley, not been drunk. When he found he could not stop the Indians from their plans to attack he first sent a message to General Claiborne; later he sent messengers to the fort itself. The guards reported these warnings to the commander but were punished for "imagining" such a story and at least one Negro was severely beaten for reporting the Indians' warning.

Red Eagle said he was surprised to find the fort in the condition it was in, but he was unable to restrain the Indians after the first shots were fired. During a lull of about one hour he attempted to talk them into leaving the fort but they refused and even threatened his life if he interfered.

Jim Cornells had left Fort Mims on the morning of August 30 and ridden some miles up river. Before noon he returned and halting at the fort gate shouted that the Indians were coming. In the argument that followed Major Beasley ordered Cornells arrested but the scout wheeled his horse and started for Fort Pierce. He yelled back once more that the Indians were coming, that if they would prepare to defend themselves he could take care of himself. But it seems that more of the garrison than Major Beasley were drunk on that day.

Later Cornells said, "Surely nowhere else in American history can an example be found where a fort was so poorly guarded, where a massacre was so needless."

T. H. Ball wrote in his book, *Fort Mims*, "This fearful massacre, one of the bloodiest in our land, has been placed at the beginning of the Creek War and its responsibility laid almost entirely upon Weatherford quite long enough. It is time that the real responsibility should be placed where it belongs."

And so perhaps those persons who believe the spirits of Chief Red Eagle and Major Daniel Beasley still are restless, still concerned with justifying their roles in the disaster should base their reasoning on solid history.

Boone told me, "Red Eagle did not want to lead the attack. History proves he was forced into it against his wishes. He knew most of the people in the fort. Beasley ignored the warnings of an impending attack. Those drumbeats over the east gate that we heard that night could have had something to do with the signals. Who can tell?"

Boone believes his illustrious ancestor would like the record set straight, that he, Chief Red Eagle, was not the villain, that he did not want to attack but was driven by pressures of the times.

Boone wonders, "Would the spirits of the massacred at Fort Mims, most of whom were friends of Red Eagle's and well known to him, be able to rest in peace if the truth were made known? Maybe they are trying to tell us the truth about what really happened at Fort Mims...and why."

The Haunted Capitol
by Kathie Farnell

March 1996

*Does a Civil War widow still stalk the halls of
the capitol in an attempt to find where her husband's body was buried?*

When a flock of Egyptian scarab beetles flew in from
nowhere and started eating the dome of the Alabama
state capitol, workers renovating the stately 150-year-
old building thought they'd seen everything.

They hadn't.

Before the $33 million renovation was completed,
they would be called upon to deal with a spectral
woman, a haunted clock, a flock of chickens, and a cat
who may have been the reincarnation of a governor.

And, of course, the scarabs.

When the beetles appeared in late 1991, architect Bill Woodsmall was surprised, but not worried. He had other problems. The renovation had dragged on for six years and the cost of the project had mushroomed from the original $4 million estimate. Woodsmall thought the beetles would go away. They didn't. They were eating the roof, a rubber membrane installed to help waterproof the dome.

Rubber, a natural material, sometimes attracts insects, but usually bugs leave when the rubber cures. This time they didn't. The scarabs, considered holy by the ancient Egyptians, kept coming back; the attacks were worst in spring but eventually the building was plagued by the bugs every day that the temperature climbed above freezing. Woodsmall ordered an additional pesticide coating for the roof, but almost four years after the first attack, the beetles are still there. Every day a worker climbs out onto the dome, checks for scarabs, and, if they're there, sprays them.

Then there was the ghost. One night in early 1992, worker James Gammage was doing decorative painting in an elevator on the second floor, when he saw the figure of a woman in Victorian dress sweep down the hall and vanish. Gammage reported to custodian Billy Misseldine that while he was willing to work long hours on the job during daylight, he would no longer work nights in the building. Misseldine was sympathetic. He had also heard footsteps and voices.

The disturbance seemed to center on the second floor in the area that had been the old Lieutenant Governor's office. Once, Misseldine clearly heard voices in the office. When he looked in, it was empty, but the telephone was off the hook.

When the renovators checked back through capitol records, they found an account of a Civil War widow, a tragic lady who stalked the halls of the capitol through the 1870s and 1880s, begging officials to help her find where her husband's body had been buried.

Misseldine doesn't know whether the apparition seen by Gammage was the Victorian widow or not. Personally, he's more concerned about the clock. A clockmaker by avocation, he had taken all the old clocks out of the building and had them repaired. The heavy marble mantel clock from the second floor governor's office was working when he replaced it on the mantel, directly under the painting of Confederate president Jefferson Davis. That night it stopped at 6:10. Misseldine examined it, wound it, and put it back on the mantel. Again, it stopped at 6:10. Since then, sometimes it works and sometimes it doesn't, but when it stops, it's always at 6:10. Once Misseldine entered the office to find the clock with its case open and the heavy glass lens cracked. He repaired it, but the clock still stops at 6:10.

A flock of chickens showed up in the building at roughly the same time the ghost was spotted. No one knows where they came from, but a clerk who has a farm took them home. About this time, workers noticed a pregnant tortoiseshell cat who seemed at home in the building. She was a sweet-natured creature. They named her Lurleen, after the state's only woman governor, Lurleen Wallace, who died in office in 1968. Temperamentally the opposite of her fiery politician husband, George Wallace,

Governor Lurleen was a shy, conscientious woman who dreaded public appearances. Elected to serve as a figurehead for her husband, she instead took her duties seriously. Her efforts to improve conditions for the state's poor people undermined her health and probably contributed to her early death from cancer. Seeing the little tortoiseshell cat's proprietary air toward the capitol offices, some workers said this was Lurleen Wallace, come back to finish her term.

Lurleen the cat and her kittens have long since been adopted, and the capitol today is maintained as a museum. Tour guides are happy to discuss the building's history, including its ghosts.

They don't mention the beetles.

The Face in the Courthouse Window

by Becky Elder

June 1996

When lightning illuminates this window, you can clearly see Henry Wells looking out, keeping his promise to haunt the townsfolk until the end of time.

People from all over the United States and around the world travel to the small western Alabama town of Carrollton to see a windowpane. This otherwise ordinary piece of glass, part of an attic window on the north side of the Pickens County courthouse, is imprinted for all time with the terrified face of a man condemned to die nearly 120 years ago. The face in the courthouse window has become one of Alabama's most popular spooky sights.

Located a few miles northwest of Tuscaloosa in the rolling farmland of western Alabama, Carrollton is almost a place out of time. Although cars have replaced horses and wagons on the road that circles the town square, footpaths have given way to sidewalks, and parking meters have replaced hitching posts, Carrollton looks much as it did 120 years ago. The buildings on the perimeter of the town square, though modernized inside, are the same ones that witnessed the tragic incident described in this article. Many Carrollton citizens are descendants of the people involved.

Here is what legend says happened: On the night of November 16, 1876, the courthouse burned to the ground in one of the largest fires ever seen in that vicinity. The building, including all the books and records in the probate office and most of the records in the sheriff's and clerk's offices, was completely destroyed. Nobody believed the fire was accidental.

In 1878, according to *The History of Pickens County* by James Clanahan, a man named Bill Burkhalter was arrested in connection with another matter. Burkhalter told the county law enforcement officers that he and a black man named Henry Wells had broken into the old courthouse that night. Wells had lit some candles in the probate office. As they left, Wells bragged that he had "set the damned thing on fire."

Burkhalter told the officers where to find Henry Wells. They arrested Wells on January 29, 1878, and returned him to Carrollton the next day to stand trial for arson. Clanahan's history contains a transcript of Wells' written confession, dated January 30. The outcome of this incident makes one wonder if Wells was truly aware of the content of the paper to which he set his mark. Other accounts of the story relate that Wells vehemently denied taking any part in the arson, maintaining his innocence until the end of his life, and, many say, beyond.

Because other episodes of vandalism had occurred during the same time period as the courthouse burning, on February 2 some of the townspeople decided to take matters into their own hands. A lynch mob gathered on the town square just outside the new courthouse, determined to carry out their own brand of justice. To prevent a lynching and to ensure that Wells would have a proper trial, the sheriff hid him in an attic room on the north side of the courthouse.

But that did not stop the mob. As they congregated on the square late that fateful afternoon, they were so focused on their goal that even the threat of a violent thunderstorm did not discourage them. Legend says that throughout the evening, Wells continually shouted down to the crowd, "I'm innocent. I didn't do it. If you kill me, I'll haunt you 'til the end of time."

We can only speculate what Wells must have felt as he looked down onto the lawn, watching the people milling around with their torches, arguing with the sheriff, threatening to rush the courthouse. As Wells pressed his face close to the glass, without warning an unusually powerful burst of lightning flashed just outside the garret window, startling everyone. The mob finally dispersed, vowing to hold the hanging the next day.

But they never got to lynch Henry Wells, for he died sometime before the next morning. Some versions of the story say he was actually lynched, others say he died in jail, and others state that he was killed in the early morning hours during a botched escape attempt.

A few days afterward, as the citizens of Carrollton looked up toward the window where Wells had been kept, much to their horror they again clearly saw his face against the glass looking back at them reproachfully as they went about their day-to-day business. They knew he was dead. They had buried him. If he had been innocent, he certainly was keeping his promise to haunt them.

The sheriff lugged many buckets full of water up the courthouse stairs to try to clean the pane, but it was no use. Throughout the years people have used all the latest techniques to try to erase the image, but nothing has worked. The face of Henry Wells, still reflecting his sorrow and anguish from that long-ago night, is etched onto the pane as clearly as a photograph.

According to a Pickens County sheriff's deputy, the pane is original and has never been replaced. A large hailstorm which came through Carrollton earlier this century broke every windowpane in the courthouse except the one with the face of Henry Wells. Every other pane in the courthouse has been replaced at some time or another.

Perhaps this phenomenon is not a ghost, but a sort of lightning-induced photograph? The locals swear that on those moonless, windswept nights when thick rain clouds ride through the sky on wild scudding storms, the kind you find only in the South, when lightning illuminates this window, you can clearly see Henry Wells looking out onto the lawn, enduring once again the misery and torment of his last night on Earth, keeping his promise to haunt the townsfolk until the end of time.

ARKANSAS

20 YEARS LATER
By Dan Thomas Howe

December 1989

*Whatever is there refuses to leave! Whatever is
there is still felt by all who visit the old house.*

Massive oak trees line the property of the two-story
house that sits on the lush, green lots just northeast of
DeWitt, Arkansas. It is here that numerous paranormal
occurrences have been prevalent for over 20 years.

The occurrences are varied, and almost unpre-
dictable in nature. There is more than the "bumps in the
night" or the "poltergeist experiences" normally associated with hauntings. This haunting defies rational explanation—or does it?

In the 1960s, the house was purchased with money
received in an accident settlement that left a boy, Francois,

near death, and his cousin Jonathan dead. The boys were riding their bicycle along U.S. Highway 165, just west of DeWitt, when a drunk driver topped a hill and plowed, head-on, into them. The cousin, riding on the handlebars of the bicycle, died instantly. Francois was terribly injured and lay near death in a Little Rock area hospital. It was months before his family told him of Jonathan's death.

By the time Francois was released from the hospital, the final arrangements were being made for the purchase of the house. Francois was 12 years old (the same age as Jonathan had been) when the family moved into the house. It wasn't very long until the family came to the realization that the house harbored much more in its confines than they had ever expected.

The father and mother, Geoff and Edan, moved Francois, his four sisters, and his brother into the house. The children were given the upstairs bedrooms, while the parents took the one downstairs.

The children, ranging in ages from 11 to 19 were the first to experience the many personalities the house had. The children told their parents about the visit they had received from "an old lady with green eyes and a flowing bath robe" who visited their bedrooms. The old lady never spoke, but sat quietly at the foot of their beds and looked at them with her green eyes glowing in the darkness. Then she simply rose silently and glided into nothingness. The parents dismissed the children's report as active imaginations at first.

After only three months in the house, the mother, Edan, became convinced that the children's stories were very real. She became frightened, but not hysterical. Whatever it was in the house seemed to pose no imminent danger to the family. Edan felt this, yet she couldn't explain why.

One warm, sultry summer morning at 6:00, Edan sat in her sprawling dining room enjoying her morning cup of coffee. The birds sang cheerfully on the limbs of the huge oak tree just outside the dining room window and the sun was peering above the tree-line that bordered her property. The bird-song was interrupted by silence, absolute silence. Edan heard 20-year-old Carolyn calling "mama," in a voice that expressed sheer horror. Carolyn came bounding down the staircase. Her skin was pale, very pale. She said, "Mama, it's talking to me and following me." Edan rose quickly to her feet and grabbed Carolyn.

"What are you saying?" Edan asked.

Carolyn replied, still hysterical, "He is right behind me, Mama!"

Edan turned and saw nothing; however, she heard the sound of footsteps approaching. The footsteps could only be described as the sound of wet feet on linoleum.

The sounds were getting closer. Edan remembered her great-grandmother telling her, when Edan was a child, that ghosts couldn't hurt people, but they could cause people to hurt themselves. She also remembered her great-grandmother saying to address the dead by saying "In the name of God, what do you want?" She told Carolyn to address the man in this way. When Carolyn did so, she turned to her mother, even more hysterical, and said, "Oh my God, Mama. He answered me!" With that Carolyn fainted.

Immediately, Edan looked at the spot where Carolyn had addressed the presence and said, "In the name of God, leave us now!" The footsteps seemed to walk back to the staircase and fade away as it climbed the stairs.

Upon waking, Carolyn could remember nothing about what had happened to her earlier that morning, perhaps from fright.

Many things began to happen after the occurrence with Carolyn. Poltergeist-like presences would unplug the family television, while the family sat in the living room watching it. The large window-fan would also stop running, as though unseen hands forcefully stopped the blades. Francois' blankets would be violently pulled off of him while he tried to rest in bed. Each time the blankets would be neatly folded at the foot of the bed, instantaneously, by unseen hands.

It is important to note at this time that Geoff and Edan Lacuaren (not their real names) and their children were very poor people. They had no material or monetary wealth. All they collected from the accident was spent on the purchase of their home. They couldn't even afford to remodel and modernize the 100-year-old structure, except for a little here and a little there. Even then, Geoff did the work.

A preacher once stated, after visiting the house with me, that there appeared to be a "dark cloud" that hung over the house, even on the sunniest days. Of course, not in the literal sense, but nonetheless, it was there.

Most of the activity centered around the children, as is typical of many poltergeist hauntings. Just prior to each experience, the air became heavy, and in daylight hours, the birdsong would cease.

The phenomena seemed to be a melange of historical periods. Some of the phenomena were apparently from the 1800s, while others were clearly in the automobile era.

Take for example the old lady. This ghostly figure was described as looking like something out of the late 1800s or early 1900s.

Another phenomenon was a car that would drive up and blow the horn at the front door. Each time the family looked for the automobile, they would find that nothing was there.

As the years passed and the children became young adults, the events became less frequent, but more bizarre.

In 1976, I was spending the night with the family. (They were my cousins and close friends.) I had always heard that something occupied the house with Edan's family, but frankly I was a skeptic. After that night, I'll never be skeptical again.

As I climbed into the bed, I noticed the area around me became very cold. Francois turned to me and said, "Oh God, it's here again!" Not knowing what to expect, like Francois in the next bed, I sat up and waited for the inevitable. What followed is something I will never forget.

On the floor of the room, we saw a faint spherical cloud of pure white that appeared to pulsate. The sound emanating from the cloud was distinctly the cry of an infant. The baby's cries became louder and louder, eventually filling the entire house. Edan appeared in the doorway of the bedroom and listened. Then she covered her face with her hands and lowered her head. The crying lasted for over 30 minutes and faded as quickly as it had begun.

This year I will celebrate my 35th birthday. Recently, I spoke with Edan, who now lives in the sprawling house all alone. (Her husband died of cancer last year.)

When I asked her if the events still occurred at the house, she replied, "Yes, it is still here, but it doesn't bother me as much anymore. Maybe I've accepted it, maybe I'm too old to worry about it, but it is still here with me."

She told me that her children visit her often, but each one of them refuses to sleep upstairs. In fact, they refuse to even go upstairs. As the children gather for the holidays, they lie on the floor of the living room in their sleeping bags and listen to the movement of furniture and the footsteps of the man in the two upstairs rooms. At times, they still hear the baby crying, as though it is being severely beaten.

The house is deteriorating with age, yet far from dilapidated. The massive oak trees seem to be drooping ever closer to the ground and the cloud still hangs over the house and property.

Whatever is there refuses to leave. Whatever is there is still felt as it makes its presence known to all who come to see.

Edan really doesn't live alone, but she doesn't know who it is she lives with, or rather, what lives with her.

Poltergeist or Prankster?
by John C. Ross

April 1962

The farm boy confessed to playing pranks—but could he really make books, cans, and biscuits float through the air?

For a while last December it looked like the country had another authentic poltergeist case on its hands. It had all the earmarks, all the mystery! Then it was blown sky high when a 15-year-old boy confessed he had done it all himself.

But had he? Some of his friends and neighbors have at least a few doubts.

It all began on the C. E. (Ed) Shinn farm near Mena, Arkansas, a year before it first received general publicity on December 2. The Shinns didn't report it for a long while because they were afraid people would "think we were crazy."

Mr. Shinn is a sturdy 72-year-old man, still actively farming on his place three miles east of Mena on Ransom Road. He and his wife, Birdie, 70, and their 15-year-old grandson, Charles Elbert Shaeffer, live in the five-room farmhouse where the events took place. The Shinns have lived in this house for 15 years and in the area for 46 years.

The unusual activities began a year before with a rattling of the windows and a knocking on the walls, like someone was trying to come in. The windows rattled as if the glass might fall out and there was another noise, too—like a man using a handsaw. The latter noise seemed to be coming from between the walls over the head of the bed.

Sheriff Bruce Scoggin of Polk County and two of his deputies, a State Police trooper, and four reporters spent a night in the house but nothing happened—the Shinns had gone to spend the night with relatives.

There were outside witnesses to some of the goings-on. Mrs. W. E. Shinn, a daughter-in-law, said she saw a coal bucket and some ears of corn sailing toward her.

Gene Whittenberg, a brother of Mrs. Shinn, declared he saw a can of dog food and a pencil in midair.

A son-in-law, J. D. Wilhite, claimed he "heard it whistle. It makes a sound like whistling at a girl sometimes and the Bob White whistle sometimes."

A neighbor, J. L. Ply, was on hand once to watch matches fly off the shelf. "I talked to a smart fellow about this thing and he told me it might be caused by uranium brought in through their well," Mr. Ply said.

Mrs. Shinn wasn't buying everything—especially the reports of all visitors. "Why, they even say that our mailbox has been revolving," she said.

Meanwhile, the Shinns added to their report. Biscuits in the kitchen were reported to have floated into the living room. Figurines were swept off a shelf in the living room and banged into Mr. Shinn's head.

Mr. Shinn fixed "it" once. When a sack of marbles belonging to Grandson Charles was scattered all over a bedroom he gathered the marbles up and put them between two bales of hay. "They haven't bothered us since," he said.

Shinn said they were awakened one night by howling and hissing noises. Mrs. Shinn asked it to be quiet but it kept right on. Then she asked it to go to sleep.

"I don't sleep," came the reply.

Then will you let me sleep?" Mrs. Shinn asked

"You don't need to sleep either," the thing answered.

But alas, many if not all good "things" must end and they say this particular "thing" turned out to be Grandson Elbert Shaeffer.

He admitted to it only a few days after his pranks had achieved nationwide publicity—confessed, yes, he had thrown chairs, marbles, and books, overturned and rearranged furniture, and made mysterious noises.

"I didn't mean to hurt no one," he sobbed to Sheriff Bruce Scoggin. "I'm sorry for all the trouble I caused."

The boy said he started the noises as a prank when he was 11 years old because "Grandpa was pickin' on me. I didn't mean for it to get out of hand, but I didn't know how to stop," he said.

The boy is a superior student in school and said he was relieved it was all over. He didn't do it anymore, he said, "because a voice told me not to."

He gave a detailed account of how he had manipulated the pranks. Some of the noise was made by tapping on the steel frame of his bed with a pair of pliers. At night, he threw things from one room to the other. He pulled the covers away from his grandparents in the dark.

He did not, he said, rattle any windows. "The wind must have done that."

That would seem to end the story of the Arkansas poltergeist, except that not everyone is convinced.

Lucius Farish, a reader of Plumerville, Arkansas, wrote FATE that "the only trouble is, nobody believes the explanation given—at least, no one familiar with poltergeist manifestations."

There was no explanation for the daytime observations, for instance, or for the reports from friends and relatives of the Shinns.

Charles Albright, columnist for the *Arkansas Gazette* of Little Rock, expressed this view in detail in his column, "Our Town."

"Anyone who takes comfort in the 'confession' of Elbert Shaeffer, the grandson, that he was the one who whipped up all the weird doings in the farmhouse near Mena either didn't read far enough or simply can't face the facts.

"Elbert says 'I did it', and everybody jumps to believe him.

"And then he adds, 'I stopped because a voice told me not to,' and what does everybody do? They have jumped clear out of earshot. It would serve them right if they landed on a stingin' snake.

"Personally we are having no part of the confession. Elbert can't make biscuits float through the air any more than we can. Hurtle through the air, maybe, or zip, but not float—not even the kind that grandmothers make.

"And what about the ears of popcorn wafting through the room in front of the coal bucket: Perhaps they wafted through in the reverse of this. It does not matter. Elbert could not have 'wafted' either.

"Our theory is that he took the rap so that everybody could get some peace. If not, what about all the eyewitnesses to the ghostly goings-on—people who didn't even live in the house. Where does this leave them? On the way to California or some place?"

FLORIDA

The Ashley's Restaurant Investigation
by Loyd Auerbach

July 1994

At Ashley's Restaurant in Rockledge, Florida,
the people are friendly and the food is excellent.
The spirits are good, too!

Ashley's Restaurant sits on highway U.S. 1 in Rockledge, Florida. Since it was built in the 1920s, the restaurant has changed names several times. It also has had a number of ghost sightings, and incidents of odd phenomena, and even odder witness reactions.

We discovered Ashley's while filming *Haunted America*, a TV pilot that featured Martin Caidin. The show is produced by Jude Gerard Prest and David

Abbitt, two independent Southern California producers. Real, ongoing investigations are featured that focus upon haunted places and the investigators themselves.

The investigative team for the show included Barbara Gallagher, Associate Director of the Office of Paranormal Investigations, a three-man team from Florida's Center for Paranormal Studies, Russ McCarty, R. Andrew Nichols, James Bosworth, and me. Caidin joined us as part of the team investigating Ashley's in June 1993.

"I've had experiences with Ashley's dating back to my days with Sybil Leek, although the restaurant had another name back then," said Caidin. "The place was a center for local paranormal activity. In those days—perhaps 20 years ago—Ashley's had a large main dining room with a large bar at one end, so there was a huge area for dinner parties." The place today has the downstairs as a bar/lounge with two side dining rooms, and a main dining room upstairs.

The first time Caidin and Sybil Leek walked through the place, she calmly announced that she felt a presence throughout the place that affected the lights in the main dining room. "Just as quickly, a coldness settled everywhere in the room, making my skin crawl as though the draft blew right through my clothes," continued Caidin. Sybil turned slowly and pointed. "It is right there."

Caidin was amazed at what happened next. While the place was being cleaned, the tables were stacked against the wall, and the chairs were upended on top of the tables. "As we watched, one chair silently rose slowly from its table, almost leisurely, and rotated. It moved to room center, then settled quietly with its legs down to the floor.

"Sybil stared directly at the still chair," said Caidin. She then told it "thank you," and led the way out of the restaurant. "It was extraordinary."

Caidin told us about another time Sybil was in the place. A chair rose off the floor, flew across the room, and smashed against the wall. He had also gathered more recent stories. "Every time I go back there, people want to talk to me about recent events."

The restaurant was written up as "The Haunted Powder Room" in Arthur Myers' *The Ghostly Registry* (Contemporary Books, 1986). Myers' book hypothesizes that the ghosts are a woman who died about 50 years ago, last seen in the restaurant wearing 1920s garb, and a spirit of a young girl killed in an auto accident on U.S. 1 just outside the restaurant.

Based on Caidin's recommendation, we selected Ashley's as a location for shooting part of *Haunted America*. Caidin, Nichols, Gallagher and I headed to Rockledge to interview witnesses, and to check the place out with special equipment that had been rented.

Owner Gregg Parker had spread the word efficiently for us and we interviewed a number of people, including current and former employees, as well as locals who had been going to Ashley's for years.

Former employee James Turner told us that sometimes when the place was closed they'd get word from the Rockledge Police Department that the lights, kitchen appliances, and power tools would come on, despite there being no one there. In addition, he witnessed glasses flying all over the place, and one occasion when "all the extinguishers went off by themselves."

Former employee Edwin Huff heard "a high-pitched scream, but it was from afar, from a distance. It seemed that the closer that I got the farther it got away from me."

Bartender Laurie Harrell has had a number of experiences there, including one night when she was closing up. "I have to go and lock all the doors. I bolt them, because I'm in here all alone." She went in the back to get beer to restock the bar. "As I was coming back into the first runway as you come in here, I felt kind of a cool breeze and saw the front door swinging open. I thought 'Oh, I've just been robbed' or something and put the beer down. I went running over to the door and there was nobody there. The door swung back, quite quickly as I was standing there and almost hit me in the face."

Martin Caidin's good friend Ken Larson told us of the experience of a friend of his who "had gone into the ladies' room. She sat down and the window that's there slowly opened up. So she stood up, she closed it, she latched it, she sat back down. It slowly opened up again. She got a little bit upset. She slammed it shut, latched it, checked it, and sat back down. This time it slammed back open.

"She ran out of the bathroom and told the person she was with, 'Pay the bill, we're getting out of here,' and she won't set foot back here again. I tried to get her down, but no way, she's not coming back here again for all the money in the world."

The ladies' room apparently is a focus of much of the goings-on at Ashley's. Our own experience there certainly proved this.

Edwin Huff, when working at Ashley's a few years ago, had an unusual experience while cleaning the ladies' room one morning before opening up. "I usually came in early in the morning. The first thing I would do was turn the lights on in the kitchen. I would always get my cleaning products and start for the powder room, the ladies' room. As I went in there one morning, I noticed that I needed tissue on one roll, and the other roll was full. So I went out to get another roll of tissue. I came back and tissue was frantically spinning off the spool by itself. No one else was in the place. There's only one window and it was closed."

Laurie Harrell told us of an incident involving the ladies' room. The girlfriends of two bikers who were at the bar went into the ladies' room together. A few moments later, the bar patrons heard them scream, and watched as they came running out of the rest room. They said something to their biker companions, and the customers and employees watched with interest as the burly guys bravely went into the ladies' room to check it out. A moment later, they too came running out, and hustled their girlfriends out of the place, never to return.

What did they see? We may never know, but perhaps they saw the ghost of a woman who may be haunting the place. According to the account in Myers' book and to some of the witnesses we interviewed, a number of people over the years have seen the image of a woman dressed in 1920s garb appear in the ladies' room. She materializes in one of the toilet stalls or in the rest room mirror.

For the investigative team of Caidin, Gallagher, Nichols, and myself (as well as our director Jude Prest and cameraman Victor J. Pancerev), when darkness fell, Ashley's began to cause problems for us.

Our video and sound equipment had been working perfectly on the job until we began our after-dark tour of the place with our sensing equipment set up. We got unusual readings on our Tri-Field meters in the magnetic range, occasional anomalies on the microwave sensor and Geiger counter, and malfunctions of our video setup, including a sound system that faded in and out. The most consistent problem we faced as we walked around (though not when we stayed put in a back room where we conducted our interviews) was the draining of our Betacam batteries.

According to Pancerev, a professional videographer (and to others in the industry I have since questioned), fully-charged batteries don't drain in less than five minutes. In addition, everything had been checked out completely before the after-dark shoot, outside the building. Unfortunately for us, our batteries didn't know that, and we had to scramble to get footage as we toured the place.

"We had batteries heating up and burning out left and right for no apparent reason. Based on past and current experiences here I say this place has some kind of energy vortex. I rest my case on the batteries. It shouldn't be happening—but it is," said Caidin.

We decided to set up the rented infrared Thermograph Video equipment in the ladies' room. Andy Nichols is fully rated to work this equipment that is mainly used for medical purposes.

It converts heat patterns to light and color patterns. This allows for viewing the hot and cold spots in the human body (you may recall this kind of heat-image video from motion pictures such as *Predator*).

We had hypothesized that such equipment would enable us to see the cold spots that so many people report in haunting situations. We had already seen evidence that the thermograph was doing more than we had expected in the other case we shot for *Haunted America*, when unusual heat fogs and energy bursts showed up for which there was no explanation.

We set the video and other equipment. Prest took the mostly used tape out of the deck, which we had just used to interview Caidin. He labeled it as "Tape 3" and unwrapped a fresh tape. Pancerev placed the tape in the deck and started it up. The red light went on, and it began recording.

They got up and headed to the ladies' room. I watched the deck to make sure it was still recording.

While Nichols, Barbara Gallagher, Prest and Pancerev were in the ladies' room, I sat watching the monitor that showed what the thermograph was picking up.

With me was Caidin's friend Mike Howard, along with Caidin and a number of others. Our Betacam setup was focused on the monitor as well, in order to record what might show up.

Mike Howard, and then I, saw what looked like a head-shaped spot of darkness, which on the thermograph meant a cold spot. That quickly vanished. Then, suddenly, I saw something a bit different as Nichols yelled from the ladies' room, "Do you see that?"

What we saw on the monitor was what looked like a cylindrical object floating in mid-air. It was not solid, but fairly well defined, and, if the thermograph was to be believed, it was much hotter than the warm air in the confined rest room.

The object seemed to be floating through the air. Nichols was able to follow it with the thermograph video and suggested that Gallagher try to move her hand to follow it so that it would contact it. "At one point," said Gallagher, "it appeared that it began to follow my hand. I felt a very slight tingling sensation, but certainly not hot as the thermograph indicated."

For me and the others watching the monitor, there was incredible excitement as we watched this object maneuver around her hand, then move away completely, looking for all the world like it was melting into the wall.

Prest, Gallagher, Nichols, and Pancerev came running out of the ladies' room so that we could run back the tape and watch what we had gotten. Then things got weirder.

Pancerev looked down at the video deck and saw that it was off. There had been no audio warning of the battery running out and when we checked it, it was still charged. "Maybe it just turned off," said Prest. Pancerev ran the tape back a bit, and we were all puzzled. It seemed to rewind quite a bit more than the few minutes we had shot on the fresh tape.

He started the deck to play and we were surprised to see Caidin's face appear on the screen. Prest stopped the deck and took out the unlabeled tape, which was almost full. He pulled out the newly labeled "Tape 3" and put it in the deck. Caidin's interview again! We had no tape of the thermograph session.

All three of us were astounded. Prest placed the labeled tape in his bag, and replaced the unlabeled one. Pancerev fast-forwarded to the end of the Caidin interview and checked the tape. There was five minutes of blank tape left. We decided to try again with the thermograph.

The deck was started again, and Prest, Pancerev, Gallagher, and Nichols headed off. Unfortunately, nothing unusual happened this time.

When Prest rewound the tape to watch the uneventful session, we were again surprised, but this time because it rewound five minutes and stopped. Pancerev pulled the tape out. It was rewound to the start. He put it back in the deck and played it. It was the second thermograph session, followed by blank tape. The Caidin interview had vanished from the tape. If this had not happened to all three of us, any one of us would have questioned the events.

The remainder of the evening was not quite as eventful, but still exciting. We took photos, some with two Polaroid cameras. The microwave, magnetic, and radiation sensors went off, often at the same time. At those times, Nichols took shots with two Polaroid cameras. Strangely enough, although the energy escaped being videotaped, we got unusual light displays on three Polaroid shots, all linked to times the other sensors had registered something at the same time.

Ashley's has become the perfect case of what can go right and go wrong on a case. While we saw the abnormalities with our own eyes (and registered them on our equipment), because of the malfunctioning video we have little in the way of a record of these things happening. Prest, as director-producer on site, was thrilled with what was happening, yet extremely frustrated that we couldn't really document it.

Even with the video equipment problems, Ashley's is a place that yielded more phenomena than any other case I had been on for a one-time visit.

And what about that cylindrical object we saw on the thermograph? Was it some form of an energy vortex? Or was it a ghost or spirit? Or maybe, as Kathy Reardon, a psychic we work with, has suggested, what we saw was the shape of the ghost's consciousness.

We hope for a return visit in the near future. In the meantime, our entire group can highly recommend a visit to Ashley's. The people are friendly and the food is excellent.

And the spirits are good, too.

The Ghost of Odka

by Arthur I. Ebbets

October 1993

A young woman's ghost befriends a Florida family.

In May of 1965 I left my work in submarines in Connecticut because the New England shore climate was having a bad effect on my wife, Lilli's, respiratory problems. With our son, Sky, we took temporary quarters as I settled into a job at Jacksonville Shipyards in Florida.

A short while later Lilli found a nice cottage on the beautiful Ortega Peninsula which juts into the St. John's River, on the west side of town. We drove by at dusk so we could see where it was and what it looked like. I agreed it was a wonderful neighborhood, but commented that the house sure looked spooky with the trees in the front yard just dripping with streamers of Spanish moss.

The next day, after getting the key from the landlord, a local doctor, we entered the house and I remarked on the odor of formaldehyde and said that perhaps the doctor had stored some such chemical there (embalming fluid?). We returned to the house a couple of hours later with our first load of furniture and thought it very strange that now there was the smell of perfume in the house.

Within the next month, we got to know our new neighbors. We shared a common driveway with them. They were Robert Truxton, a chief aviation machinist's mate, his wife, and three children. Lilli became friendly with Mrs. Truxton, who confided to my wife about strange things going on in their house. They did not use the upstairs as the children were afraid to sleep there.

One evening, right after they moved in, they were all in the living room watching TV, with the door to the front hall closed to limit the area being cooled by their window air conditioner. They suddenly heard the front door open and close, and footsteps go upstairs. Mr. Truxton jumped out of his chair, went to the hall and up the stairs and through the upstairs rooms and down the long fire escape which extended straight out into the back yard, but found no one. This happened almost every night for quite a while, and after half a dozen fruitless chases, they tried to ignore it.

The Truxtons made cautious inquiries of longtime nearby residents and learned that three or so years before, a German couple had owned the Truxton house, the house we occupied and the house beyond the lawn-covered lot beside the middle house. They had been killed in an auto accident, leaving the properties to their twenty-one-year-old daughter, who had the unlikely name of Odka Grother.

It is probable that Odka, after a year on her own, was not handling her responsibilities or her life very well, with both boyfriends and girlfriends staying over. One day, when a boyfriend was at the clothesline in the backyard, both he and a neighbor, just over the back fence, heard a shot ring out upstairs. Odka had committed suicide.

Shortly after Lilli, Sky and I settled in, Mrs. Truxton's mother came to visit her and had to sleep upstairs in Odka's former room. She had to endure having the bed covers pulled off and the light turned on frequentiy all night. Odka must have wanted her bed. This was a brave woman because she came back and slept there on two more occasions with fewer disturbances.

The ghost of Odka showed herself on only one occasion that I heard of. The family in the third house was standing in their back yard conversing with friends when, 130 feet across the vacant lawn, all five of them saw Odka come down the fire escape in the gray nightgown she was wearing when she died. As she reached the ground, her image faded away.

Although Odka's presence was never, to my knowledge, felt in that third house, she was often in the cottage we rented. She was no doubt there on day one and made the accommodating odor change.

Her presence was first physically noticed by my son who was going to sleep one night and called out, "Mom, someone's breathing in my face."

Lilli answered, "Don't worry, Sky, that's only Odka. She loves you."

The ghost checked up on Sky a few other times and the only time he ever sleepwalked, she woke him up. In the middle of the night, Sky came running, screaming and crying, into the house. When we could make sense of him he said, "I woke up out in the driveway. I don't know how I got there. Someone was grabbing me, but there was nobody there."

My only physical contact with the spirit was this: one evening as Lilli was preparing supper in our small kitchen, I passed from the kitchen into the dining room where we always ate. I felt a sharp rap or twinge on the top right rear of my head. There are no muscles there and I was mystified as to what it could have been. It felt as though someone had struck me with the flat of their finger nail by flipping a finger off their thumb, as most of us learn to do. By the next evening, I had dismissed it, when at the same time and place, a pencil bounced off the same portion of my head.

Odka wasn't as playful with Mrs. Truxton, who was inside her enclosed back porch one day when a tree stick an inch in diameter and two feet long fell from a tree and bounced off her head.

Because the spirit seemed so friendly toward us, my wife enlisted her cooperation on several occasions. When Lilli would want to take a nap, she would say aloud, "Odka, don't let the phone ring while I'm napping." It would never ring, even though Lilli normally got a lot of phone calls.

One time Lilli had to take the city bus to the dentist and did not have the seventy cents exact change required. She said, "Odka, help me find some money," and went about the house looking in whatever odd place she seemed to be led to. She found seventy cents in two or three minutes.

The most remarkable incident happened to previous residents. One day a car pulled into the driveway between the houses while I was sitting on our front porch. I recognized the uniformed driver, who was staring at the Truxton house, to be a lieutenant commander and naval aviator as I had been. I went to the side of the porch and asked, "Can I help you?"

Just then, Lilli came out the front door and we heard him respond, "No, I used to know someone who lived here." My wife instantly surmised the reason for his visit and asked him if he would come up on the porch and talk with us a few minutes. After a half minute of silence, he agreed.

He told us, "Yes, I knew Odka very well," and then told us why he thought she might still be around.

The commander had been billeted at the Jacksonville Naval Air Station, five miles south of Ortega. He was transferred to Corpus Christi NAS in late summer of Odka's last year. In late autumn he received a phone call. The voice on the phone said, "If you know what's good for you, you'll come over to Jacksonville as soon as possible."

He asked, "Who is this?"

The answer was, "You know who this is."

He relented and said, "OK, I'll get a plane on the weekend and fly over," which he did.

He borrowed a car from a friend at JAX NAS and drove up to the house, pulled into the driveway, and went to the back door. His knock was answered by a woman he had never seen before. He asked, "Is Odka home?"

He was told, "No one here by that name."

Puzzled, he said how far he'd come and that she hadn't told him she had moved. Whereupon the lady at the door said she had heard something about the former owner having killed herself a couple of months before.

A true phone call from the dead.

Before we left Jacksonville, Lilli had her hairdresser, who did automatic writing, come out to our house. After receiving information pertinent to other matters, we asked the auto-writing communicant what we could do for Odka. The answer came, "Light candles and pray." We did as advised and hopefully, her spirit is less troubled and getting on with her existence in the next plane.

Our Ghost
Did Not Approve
By David Gray

October 1984

As hate-filled ghostly voices shrieked in her ear, she fought against an invisible force that was trying to kill her.

Soon after Starr and I met in November 1979 we fell in love. It surprised us both. I was a confirmed bachelor of 38 and she was a twenty-two-year-old divorcée. I was formal, introverted, and logical; she was matter-of-fact and outgoing and all too often let her heart over-rule her head. To top off our differences, at six-feet-four I was a foot taller than she.

We were not prepared for marriage. Differences in our backgrounds made us wary, so we decided to live together, despite disapproval from our families. Starr was studying Secretarial Occupations in St. Augustine, Florida, and I worked on my family's farm near Hastings, twenty miles away. We decided it would be most convenient to live near Starr's school and also, St. Augustine was larger than Hastings and would give us anonymity.

We answered an ad for an apartment in a huge old house called the Abbott Mansion, two blocks north of Ripley's Believe It or Not Museum. The landlady was a short, plump, dark-haired woman named Joy Parker. She was thirtyish and pleasant and we liked her on sight. To prevent complications we told her we were newlyweds.

The three-story house and enclosed grounds covered three-quarters of a city block. The first floor housed an art supply store; the second floor was divided between the apartment we had come to see and an art studio. On the third floor were two more apartments, one of which was occupied by a solitary tenant. The advertised apartment had two bedrooms, a living room and a kitchen-dinette. It was beautiful, with windows overlooking the extensive grounds and a fireplace in each bedroom.

We were puzzled by the low rent. Joy explained it matter-of-factly: "The mansion is haunted." She told us she had seen two different ghosts on many occasions. One was Miss Lucy, a member of the Abbott family who had built the mansion more than one hundred years ago. The other was a man she could not identify but she called him "the Captain" because of his seafaring garb.

Starr and I were intrigued. She feels she is sensitive to the spirit world and I have more than a passing interest in the occult—but I took Joy's descriptions with a grain of salt. After all, all old houses make noises at night. We quickly agreed we wanted the apartment—and if there was a quiet, dignified ghost about, so much the better!

On January 31, 1980, Starr, her Chihuahua Angie and I moved into the apartment, eagerly anticipating our first contact with the spirits. We didn't know what to expect and that first evening we kept looking over our shoulders and jumping at every sound. Finally I grumbled, "It doesn't look like they're going to show up."

Starr was more philosophical. "It may take them a while to get used to us," she said.

Before falling asleep I listened to the noises in the house. None of them was mysterious and I decided that Joy simply had a keen imagination. Then, at 3:30 in the morning, a loud knocking on the door of the apartment awakened me. Angie was growling.

"All right, I'm coming," I called, pulling on my pants. The only people in the house were Joy and the third-floor tenant. I couldn't imagine why either of them would want to see us but the knocking sounded urgent.

"What's the matter?" I asked as I opened the door. There was no one there. Suddenly I was wide awake. Cautiously I stepped out into the well-lighted hall. There was no place for a jokester to hide and there hadn't been time for him to use the stairs. It dawned on me that I had met one of the ghosts.

I stood in the hall for a time to see if anything would happen but everything was peaceful. When I went back to bed I found that Starr had slept through it all.

When we discussed the incident at breakfast Starr made me promise to wake her in the event of a repeat performance. I agreed but told her that it had not been exciting, merely puzzling.

That afternoon Starr met the third-floor tenant for the first time. He was moving out. Starr expressed polite regret, then asked, "Have you had any contact with the ghosts?"

He scowled. "I see you've been talking to Joy. She imagines things. I don't believe in ghosts—but this house is too much for me." With that he departed.

She was telling me about this at suppertime when a knock on the door interrupted us. Angie began to bark as I went to the door. There was no one there. Again I examined the hall carefully. I could find no way for someone to play a practical joke.

I turned back to Starr to find her visibly upset. "What's the matter, honey?" I asked.

"The things in the house, David," she whispered. "They don't like me."

I pressed for an explanation. How did she know that? She shook her head. "It's just a feeling I have."

About nine o'clock we heard footsteps in the hall. Angie began to bark again and a knock sounded on the door. Of course, no one was there.

"At least they're showing us a little variety," I told Starr. "The footsteps are new."

The knocking occurred at intervals over the next few weeks. Sometimes we heard footsteps, sometimes not. Almost always we were awakened between three and four in the morning. We came to take the knocking for granted. It was petulant, even childlike. If we didn't open the door it would continue intermittently for hours. Once the door was open, however, the knocking stopped.

While I was reading one night I heard footsteps. Without thinking, clad only in my underwear, I opened the door. To my chagrin, it was the art class leaving the studio next door.

When I returned from work the next day the apartment was empty. Both Starr and Angie were gone. I began to worry. This was not like Starr at all. By nightfall I was debating whether or not to call the police. Before I could decide Starr returned.

She was very upset. "I waited until I was sure you were here," she said. In the afternoon that day she had felt a sudden chill; then a voice, speaking in a harsh, hate-filled whisper, said, "Get out!"

"That's what I did," she concluded.

I had a man's normal reaction when someone he loves is threatened. I became belligerent. I stalked angrily around the apartment seeking an outlet for my rage. Not wanting to be alone, Starr followed me. We discovered three cold spots in the apartment, one in each bedroom and the third near the bathroom door. Later we were to find these varied from day to day in size and degree of chill.

The next day Starr was talking with Lillian, the proprietor of the art supply store downstairs, and she mentioned the spirits. Lillian readily admitted seeing things which she thought were ghosts. "They don't bother me," she said. "I put up with them because I don't stay here at night."

Later Starr told me she had had a talk with Joy. "I told her we weren't married," she confessed. "She told me she knew." Starr also told her about the voice. Joy laughed and insisted the spirits were friendly—although she admitted they could be boisterous. Two college girls, previous tenants of our apartment, had been frightened enough to leave and a pair of male college students had vacated a third-floor apartment after finding it repeatedly ransacked.

One Sunday morning I was reading the paper in bed while Starr took a bath. Suddenly she ran into the bedroom and jumped under the covers, still wet and soapy.

"It was that voice," she stammered. "I felt a chill and then it ordered me out."

I soothed her as best I could and reminded her that Joy had said the spirits were unsettling but harmless.

"It's different with you," she replied. "They like you—but I feel they hate me."

What could I say to her? When the knocks came again I was angry and challenged the spirits to show themselves. It had no effect.

We were pleased when Joy told us she had rented one of the third-floor apartments to a family with children; perhaps it would reduce some of the pressure. The first evening after they moved in we could hear them walking and talking noisily above our heads. The next day they left without giving Joy a reason.

The next time Starr heard the voice telling her to get out, she made a decision: she wouldn't enter the apartment unless I was there. These goings-on made us both irritable. One night we had a heated argument and Starr stalked off to sleep in the other bedroom. She returned a half hour later, terrified. The bed had started inexplicably shaking. The spirits had done us a good turn. We were speedily reconciled.

Next we both began to hear voices. They came from the cold spot near the bathroom door, indistinct and far away. It sounded like several people talking at once and we couldn't understand a word.

The knocking was annoying and the voices were worrisome but nothing really serious happened until one night when we had decided to go bowling. I started out first, leaving Starr upstairs. When she didn't join me I reentered the house and called up from the foot of the stairs, "Honey, we're going to be late."

"Just a second," she called back and shortly appeared at the top of the stairs. Her expression told me something was wrong. I was about to call out when suddenly she fell forward! She caught herself after falling down a few steps but she had hurt her back. I rushed her to the hospital where X-rays showed only severe bruises. There would be no bowling that night but in time she would recover.

On the way home I asked, "What made you fall, sweetheart?"

"I felt that chill so I stopped," she replied. "Then something pushed me. It felt like a hand. "

This was vicious. I was infuriated and helpless. What would the spirits do next?

Our next surprise came on Easter Sunday 1980. Starr was napping and I sat at the kitchen table, reading. Suddenly feeling as if I were being watched, I glanced around. A pale white form stood in the darkly shadowed living room. The figure was about 12 feet away from me, standing next to a wall. It was a short, plump woman wearing an old-fashioned floor-length dress with puffed sleeves and a square neckline. Wisps of stringy, graying hair showed under her white hat which was tied with a ribbon under her double chin.

Her dark eyes stared unsmilingly at me—and I stared back. She appeared to be a living, breathing person except that she was transparent. Belatedly it hit me. I was seeing a ghost. "Wow!" I cried.

The noise seemed to startle her. She moved sideways, not walking but floating, and disappeared into the wall. Starr lay asleep on the other side of that wall. She awoke when I cried out but saw nothing.

That spring, Starr and I were married. After the ceremony Starr confessed, "I couldn't tell you before because it would sound like I was trying to force you to marry me, but the spirits hated me because we weren't married. They were old-fashioned people who believed in the double standard. It was all right for a man to be living in sin but it was wrong for a woman."

Joy was happy for us. She had had the same feeling as Starr and now predicted an end to our troubles with the spirits. Things were quieter. The knocking continued but the cold spots were gone. Starr sensed a difference in the spirits. "They still don't like me," she said, "but they don't hate me."

That judgment was to prove a little premature.

Now that we were married, we discussed buying a mobile home and moving nearer Hastings where I worked. But it would be expensive and since the spirits seemed less troublesome, we put off making a decision.

One night as we were falling asleep, we became aware that there was something in the room—a dark, indefinite shape where the cold spot had been. It was composed of thin streaks, like cigarette smoke. Starr could see it more clearly than I. "It's a man," she whispered, "with dark, bushy eyebrows. He's frowning at me."

I tried but couldn't make him out; all I could see was an indefinite shape. I switched on the light—and of course there was nothing there. The spot where he had been was cold for the first time since our marriage.

Starr was upset. "They hate me again," she shivered. "I'm still a loose woman in their eyes."

The indistinct voices returned, now shrill and hostile. Something pushed Starr down the stairs again. She escaped serious injury but it was a turning point for me, the last straw. I borrowed money to buy a mobile home and we prepared to move. Starr was packing boxes and I was carrying full ones down to the truck. On one trip back upstairs I found my wife hysterical. She had leaned out the window to call down to me when an unseen hand began pushing her. She grabbed the window frame, one hand on either side, and struggled for several minutes before the spirit relented. Small wonder she was upset!

We departed without further incident, ending our contact with Abbott Mansion and the spirit world. It was the 28th of May, nearly four months after we had moved in. Since then we have told our story to many people. They react in one of two ways, either accepting everything we say with enthusiasm or kidding us about our overactive imaginations. But we know a great weight lifted from our shoulders when we moved away from those rambunctious spirits.

The Trouble with Eden
By William H. Wesley

January 1979

In the darkness we could see eerie forms dart out from under the table and move rapidly around the room before they floated upward and disappeared into the ceiling.

A white-columned mansion furnished with priceless antiques and set under a canopy of moss-draped oaks is the prime attraction in Eden State Gardens and Museum south of Defuniak Springs, Florida. Although the house was built in 1895, it has the regal splendor and graciousness of the Old South's antebellum plantation era. It was named "Eden" by Lois Maxon, a wealthy New York journalist, who bought it in 1963. After spending five years and a lot of money on its renovation she gave the mansion and gardens to the state of Florida and in the late 1960s it was opened to the public.

Visitors who tour the mansion sometimes ask the tour guide, "Has the house ever had any ghosts?" Smiling, she replies, "Yes, and it still has." Everyone in my family knows she speaks the truth, for she is talking about the house my grandfather built and where I lived as a youth.

The last time I spent a night in the one-to-two-room family home was in 1950 when I was a college freshman. I was visiting my grandmother, Katie Wesley, who had been living alone since my grandfather's death a few months earlier. I lay in bed listening to the familiar cries of whippoorwills and screech owls, the croaking of frogs and the hum of millions of insects when suddenly a sound from inside the house brought back memories of my boyhood. Heavy measured footsteps were slowly moving across the floor of the vacant room above. In the years since I had slept in the old house I had forgotten the chill that came with those eerie inexplicable sounds. While I held my breath and listened, the footfalls paused, a door closed, and the pacing steps faded down the upstairs hall.

My father, William H. Wesley, Jr., was killed in an automobile accident in June 1936 when I was five and my sister Carol only a few weeks old. Much later I learned that my father seemed to have a premonition of his death. Three days before the accident, he had had a long, serious talk with my grandmother about various matters that would need attention if anything happened to him. His main concern had been the care of his family after his death. Therefore, my mother Carlotta, my sister and I lived with my grandparents for the next nine years. In that time many mysterious things occurred.

Soon after my father's death it became a family custom in the winter to gather around the large fireplace in the living room for sessions of reading aloud. I remember well how often the reading was interrupted by footsteps sounding in the seldom-used second-floor room above, sometimes accompanied by doors slamming or the scraping of moving furniture. In the beginning Mother or Grandmother would go upstairs to investigate but they never found an explanation for the noises. Eventually it became routine to sit, wide-eyed and silent, until the racket was over; then we'd continue with the reading.

Also, on occasion, footsteps and voices were heard in the daytime. I remember a midday meal that was interrupted by footsteps sounding in the first-floor hallway and moving along the side porch. My Aunt Mabel Burlison, who lived nearby, called out a familiar greeting and then we all heard the distinct squeak of hinges and the slamming of the screen door. We waited expectantly for Aunt Mabel to enter the kitchen where we were eating but she did not come. We left the table and searched for her, thinking she was playing a joke of some sort, but we didn't find her. Later in the day Aunt Mabel did visit and was just as mystified by our experience as we were.

The second-floor room from which the noises came during our reading sessions was once occupied by boarders, a young couple named Poole. On several occasions while her husband was at work Mrs. Poole heard footsteps approaching her door, then a knock and a voice saying, "Hello." When she opened the door she found no one there. She was badly frightened by the experiences and the family had to tell her that such events were not unusual and at the same time reassure her that nothing more serious than the unwelcome noises would occur.

Manifestations other than sounds were part of the eerie events. One of these was the nocturnal appearance of fluffy white cloudlike objects about the size of basketballs, which seemed to float one or two feet above the ground. The first such object was seen by my grandmother just after the home was first completed in 1895. She was riding a horse about a mile from home just after dark when the strange fluffy ball appeared in the air ahead of her. Her horse was frightened and could not be urged forward. Grandmother told us that she dismounted, tied the horse to a tree and tried to approach the floating ball on foot. This was to no avail, however, for the mysterious form would move a few feet up or down or to either side, always remaining a fixed distance away. When Grandmother stood still the object stood still. She watched for several minutes until the form rose slowly to a height of eight or ten feet, then vanished.

About thirty years later my father encountered this phenomenon. He was driving an early-model automobile toward home after dark and traveling about twenty-five miles per hour. When he was within a mile of home he noticed two fluffy cloudlike balls following him. They were in the roadway about twenty or thirty yards behind his car and remained a fixed distance away regardless of his change of speed. Eventually Father stopped the car and tried to approach the objects on foot, as Grandmother had. His results were like hers.

The third and final encounter with these puffy balls took place in 1942. The whole family—Grandfather, Grandmother, Mother, my sister and I—were returning from an evening church service. As we entered the front yard Grandmother happened to look back, then called our attention to the two circles of white fluff floating over the road behind us. Right under our eyes the two objects suddenly streaked through the still-open gate past us and up the sidewalk, up the steps, across the front porch and into the open hallway of the house. Everyone was puzzled and apprehensive, but we slowly followed into the dark hall. At first we couldn't see anything, but as our eyes grew accustomed to the darkness all of us saw the forms dart out from under a corner table near the stairway. After performing several swift erratic maneuvers over the table and stairs they finally seemed to disappear through the ceiling.

One of my personal encounters with the unexplainable took place about a year later — in 1943 when I was 12. After I went to bed one night I heard someone walking barefooted through my darkened room. Thinking Mother was going to turn on the light and talk to me, I waited. Nothing happened for several moments; then my bed felt as if someone had sat down on its edge. I still thought it was Mother, and I spoke to her. Getting no answer I reached out to where I expected her to be. I felt only thin air. Suddenly realizing that no physical being had made the depression in my mattress, I got out of bed quickly and turned on the light. Of course there was no one there. Mother had been asleep in her own room all alone and could offer no explanation for my experience.

The final event involving my family was a dream my sister had. After the family home was sold when Grandmother died in the early 1950s, the house stood vacant for many years and fell into disrepair. During this period Carol had her dream.

Describing the dream to me, she emphasized that everything was in vivid color and realistic. Although she recognized the old family home, it was not dilapidated but shining in bright new splendor, filled with elegant furniture, and surrounded by beautiful well-kept grounds. Years later, when we first visited the house after it had been restored and the grounds landscaped, Carol reminded me of her dream and exclaimed, "This is exactly the way I saw the house in that dream!"

GEORGIA

Georgia's Supernatural Sites
by Wes Swietek

July 1996

Visitors to the Peach State can take in a whole host of supernatural sites—from haunted mansions to Georgia's own version of Stonehenge.

Many of the founders of Atlanta lie beneath a canopy of majestic oak and magnolia branches in the city's oldest public cemetery. In 1850, city officials purchased six wooded acres on the outskirts of the city to be used as a cemetery. It was named Oakland after the street that ran along its main entrance. The remains of many of those buried elsewhere were moved to the cemetery, which soon became the standard final resting place for the city's most prominent citizens.

81

The peculiar tastes of some more eccentric Atlantans are reflected in the myriad elaborate monuments, headstones, and mausoleums that fill Oakland. A large stone memorial decorated with Egyptian symbols stands guard over one family's plot; a mausoleum built to look like a gothic castle—complete with gargoyles and stained glass windows—contains the remains of another family. In one of the cemetery's newer and more conventional plots lie the remains of Margaret Mitchell, the author of *Gone With the Wind*.

But it is near the center of the cemetery that the restless dead occasionally make their presence known to visitors.

General W. T. Sherman's capture of Atlanta was a turning point in the Civil War. The siege on the city was, like the war itself, brutal and bloody. In the heat of battle, thousands of soldiers were buried in shallow pits. The ridges formed by these makeshift graves ringed the city after the war. In 1872, the bodies of 3,000 to 4,600 military dead were reburied in Oakland Cemetery.

Among the sea of small slabs marking the tombs lie graves of unidentified soldiers. A granite memorial to the unknown Confederate dead, based on the Lion of Lucerne, guards that section of the cemetery. The memorial is a massive statue of a wounded lion lying on a furled Confederate flag.

It is here, near the memorial, that visitors repeatedly have reported hearing a somber roll call: a voice not of this world calling out the forgotten names of those who died.

The cemetery, now ringed by a brick wall, lies in the heart of Atlanta. The city's downtown skyscrapers are visible from many spots in the cemetery. Oakland Cemetery is open to the public seven days a week, and tours are offered on a regular basis.

In Buford, a rural town on the fringes of metropolitan Atlanta, stands the "old telephone building," as it is known to residents. The brick, one-story building was built on the site of a house occupied by Jim Lights in the 1930s. Lights has long been dead and the building now houses offices, but the ghost of the previous owner is still hanging around.

For years, workers in the building have reported ghostly manifestations: sounds of footsteps when no one is there, slamming doors, office equipment that turns itself off and on, and a number of unexplainable noises.

Lights has been seen by at least two witnesses who gave the same description of an old man of medium height with a full gray beard. Lights reportedly died in the house. Some long-time Buford residents remember stories regarding Lights' hoarded wealth, which he refused to entrust to a bank. Some Buford residents think Lights buried the money on the property and still returns periodically to check on it.

Savannah, on the Atlantic coast, is Georgia's oldest city and home to many of the state's most noted haunted sites.

Antebellum mansions draped in Spanish moss, the town's many statue-filled squares, countless bed and breakfasts in grand old homes, and a historic, bustling business district make Savannah one of the South's most popular vacation destinations, as well as a favorite location for Hollywood filmmakers looking for a picturesque location that fits the image of the traditional South.

The city's long history has also given Savannah a wealth of legends—many associated with eighteenth-century pirates who visited Savannah's bustling port. The aptly named Pirates House restaurant, which flies the skull and crossbones above its front doors, and the Shrimp Factory are two of Savannah's most popular haunted eateries. Guests at the Kehoe House bed and breakfast have also been known to encounter ghosts.

The Kehoe House was built in 1892 by iron magnate William Kehoe. It has been used for various purposes since the family sold the home in 1930. For a time, it was a funeral parlor. More recently, the luxurious three-story home was turned into an opulent bed and breakfast. More than half-a-dozen guests have reported ghostly encounters since then. All the incidents have occurred in two rooms: 201 and 203. Some patrons have reported seeing the image of a young girl dressed in servant's clothes, while others have seen the apparition of an elderly lady wearing a shroud over her head.

Bonaventure Cemetery in Savannah also received a burst of notoriety after being featured in John Berendt's best-selling book *Midnight in the Garden of Good and Evil*. Legend recounts that the cemetery is on the site of a colonial plantation. The plantation's owner was hosting a grand party, the type for which Savannah is still known, when the house caught on fire in the middle of dinner. Host and guests simply picked up their plates and utensils and transferred the party to the mansion's grounds. As the mansion burned to its foundation in the background, the carousers ended their meal by smashing wine glasses against a tree.

Visitors to the cemetery have reported that the sounds of the revelers, as well as of the smashing of glassware, can still be heard on certain nights.

Just north of Dalton, Georgia, lies an almost-forgotten, unnamed cemetery. Most of the graves in the cemetery date back to the Civil War era and contain the remains of slaves—hence it is known as the "old black cemetery."

And while its graves are rarely visited by the living, a phantom has been repeatedly sighted by those who do come to the graveyard. Several sightings of the phantom, described as a man of medium height wearing a hooded garment, were reported in the 1970s. The phantom is reported to have a chalky white face and eyes that glow like hot coals. As new subdivisions sprang up in the vicinity of the old cemetery, unusual poltergeist-like activities began to be reported in the homes nearest the cemetery.

Along the winding Altamah River in south Georgia lies Rock Oven, a series of caves and limestone formations that once was the dwelling place of a secluded Indian tribe. The area is now widely known for being home to unusual phenomena.

Rock Oven received its unusual name because of the charred soot that covers the roofs of some of the caves. The soot is one of the still-visible reminders that the area was once the home to the Tama, a now-extinct Indian tribe about which little is known. Other evidence of Indian habitation, such as pottery shards and arrowheads, occasionally surface in the area, as do strange reports of mysterious happenings: spook lights, disembodied voices, and sightings of spectral Indians dancing around campfires.

Athens, Georgia, about 60 miles east of Atlanta, is home to the University of Georgia and many historic homes, some of them reportedly haunted.

The Taylor-Grady home, according to many witnesses, is visited every Christmas by an unidentified Confederate soldier and a female companion.

The 100-year-old Thomas-Carithers House, now home to a sorority, has a ghost legend associated with one of its rooms. A bride-to-be retreated to the room and hung herself after being left at the altar. She still occasionally makes appearances. According to legend, any woman assigned the room becomes engaged before she leaves college.

Even the University of Georgia's president's office, located in the historic Lustrat House, is home to a ghost. This ghost, one Major Morris, is known to take a seat near the fireplace on chilly evenings. His apparition has been sighted by dozens of visitors.

Near the Lustrat House lies a marker for an oak tree and a curious legend. The marker denotes the spot on which once stood a majestic oak associated with the life of Robert Toombs, a lawyer, planter, and statesman who served in Congress and the Senate.

As a young man, Toombs attended Franklin College, which would later become the University of Georgia. He was dismissed from the school in 1828 for boisterous behavior, but returned at the next commencement day and delivered a speech so eloquent that the entire audience of the commencement exercise left the ceremony to listen. He spoke under the sheltering branches of the great oak. Legend says that on the day Toombs died in 1885, the great oak at which he first came to prominence was struck by lightning. The dead tree finally collapsed in 1908 and was cut into small fragments that have been passed down from generation to generation of University of Georgia alumni ever since. A marker was erected on the site of the old oak by the state's general assembly in 1985.

One of Georgia's most unusual sites has relatively modern origins. This is the Georgia Guidestones, the monolithic formation near Elberton, a small community about 75 miles northeast of Atlanta. The Guidestones are a series of granite pillars 29 feet 3 inches tall and weighing 28 tons. They form an X pattern. The stones are astronomically aligned so that the rising and setting sun shines through a "window" in the center stone. Etched on the Guidestones are 10 commandments or religious tracts written in 12 languages, including Sanskrit and ancient Egyptian hieroglyphics.

The Guidestones were designed and paid for by an unidentified man using the pseudonym Robert C. Christian in 1970 or 1980 (there are conflicting reports). Who Christian was and why he had the Guidestones erected remains the subject of much speculation.

The site upon which the formation was built is near Al-yeh-li A lo-Hee—the center of the universe according to Cherokee Indian legends. No one is sure if the Guidestones were purposefully built near the Cherokee location, but occult powers, mysterious noises, and strange rituals have been attributed to both sites.

Haunts of Hell's Holler
By Mary Joyce Porcelli

July 1983

A remote Georgia community, named for past rowdiness, is today friendly and hospitable—but the same can't be said for its ghosts.

Hell's Holler is a small farming community which begins where the paved highway ends in a remote mountainous area of northern Georgia. The people in this backwoods community are friendly, fun-loving, and hospitable—but the same can't be said for the ghosts who live there.

On July 3, 1982, Clawson Payne's family was startled when he came back to the house, pale and shaken, only a few minutes after his 5:30 A.M. departure. He had left later than usual and his wife wondered frantically why her husband, who had not missed a day's work in fifteen

88

years, was not rushing to his job in the copper mines sixteen miles away. Clawson seemed too terrified to offer an adequate explanation. He mumbled incoherently about an automobile accident, then rushed into a bedroom and closed the door against his family's almost hysterical questions. The younger children raced outside to see the damage but except for its usual dents and scratches, the red 1964 Ford Fairlane seemed unharmed.

I was visiting the Payne family at the time of the incident and that afternoon, when Clawson related a bizarre story of "the Hell's Holler ghost pup," which he claimed had nearly caused him to lose his life, I could hardly hide my smile. Knowing Clawson's tendency to exaggerate, especially after a few nips of liquor, and realizing what a kind heart beats beneath his rough exterior, I secretly surmised he had run over a dog and was now trying to ease his troubled conscience. Because I was due at the house of another friend in Murphy, North Carolina, the next morning—a good hour's drive from Hell's Holler—I retired early that evening and temporarily forgot Clawson's strange tale.

The next day dawned bright and sunny and as I drove toward the paved highway I was thinking what perfect weather it was for an Independence Day picnic. Then, from the corner of my eye, I saw a small white blur darting toward the front wheels of my car. Hoping to avoid killing one of the neighbor's pups, I turned the wheel sharply. The car began to rock violently from side to side while the steering wheel spun wildly under my helpless hands. And although the temperature was climbing into the eighties, a strange loud wind came through the open window and whistled around my head. Before I had time to think, the ordeal was over. Everything was still again, the white form had disappeared and my car was running smoothly. I brushed down my frazzled hair with trembling hands and drove on. Later that morning I forgave my friend when she bit her lip to keep from grinning after I told her my incredible but nevertheless true story.

After having dealt personally with one of the Hell's Holler ghosts, I listened more respectfully to the numerous strange accounts. When I heard about a headless body that reportedly was seen only after midnight on a certain deserted gravel road, I decided to seek out this phenomenon myself. On July 13, 1982, I persuaded my youngest sister Edna Carr, an adventurous type, to accompany me.

Despite our brave intentions, after we had parked we were both too nervous to unlock the car doors and step outside. We waited in silence, peering at the stars. After an hour we began to feel a bit foolish and agreed it was time to give up; there seemed to be no ghost. I was ready to turn the ignition key and Edna already had closed her eyes for a nap when an invisible heavy hand began to pound slowly and rhythmically on the roof of the car. In wide-eyed shock, we looked up to see the black vinyl top of my yellow Datsun heaving up and down with each thunderous ghostly strike.

"Go!" Edna hissed, too stunned to say anything more.

As we roared out of the area, wheels spinning, one part of my mind persisted in arguing that somebody must have been near the car. I glanced into the rearview mirror—but all I saw was a small whirlwind of red dust and gravel stirred up by our sudden departure. The ghost that haunts this road apparently had not been pleased by two foolhardy women seeking adventure; I felt extremely thankful that no headless body had materialized.

My third encounter with one of Hell's Holler's supernatural beings was the most terrifying. It happened after I had sworn off ghost hunting because of the last ordeal. When an elderly family friend, a woman I knew only as Widow Sands who had lived alone for many years in a small house in one of the remotest areas of Hell's Holler, graciously invited me to spend a night during my visit, I willingly accepted, especially after the frail but independent lady laughingly informed me that "things of another dimension" were not allowed to enter her home.

That night I snuggled into the featherbed and stared drowsily at the splintered roughhewn walls, regretting that it would soon be time for me to return to city life. In no time I fell asleep—to be awakened suddenly by a strong sense of impending peril. I groped desperately in the darkness for the bedside clock; it was 3:00 A.M.

Now an invisible presence made itself known in the pitch-black room, emitting a vile, evil aura. I dropped the clock and slumped back immobile, paralyzed with fear, cold sweat beading my forehead. In desperation I tried to pray but as soon as I mouthed the first words a heavy weight began to press down on my body with painful force.

"Dear God!" I prayed, sure that soon I would suffocate under this enormous weight that I could not see. I had to get to the lamp; I knew instinctively that if I could, all would be normal again. I arched my body upward with the extraordinary strength derived from sheer panic. Freed of the supernatural burden, I raced across the cool hardwood floor and flicked the lamp switch, sobbing with relief as yellow light flooded the room. The evil fled with the darkness.

In the morning Widow Sands found me, still weeping, curled in an armchair in her well-lit living room. She sniffed in disdain at my tale and hinted darkly that my "writer's imagination" was playing havoc with my sanity.

During the last two weeks of my Georgia visit I began to wonder if she was right. Was I so convinced of the existence of Hell's Holler ghosts that I created their reality in my mind? No, for another sister—Margaret Ann Carr, by far the most levelheaded member of our family—who knew nothing of my spooky encounter, shyly confessed to a similar experience (without the crushing sensation) in Widow Sands' house a year earlier to the day—on July 21, 1981. The night of my encounter was July 21, 1982.

Legends of ghosts of times past are still echoed today in Hell's Holler. The tale of the ghost riders is a favorite with trick-or-treaters but Sue Griffith doesn't laugh with the crowd when the story is told. She heard the thundering hooves of invisible horses. In her own words:

"I was seven years old when my family lived in Hell's Holler about 1950. The main road, a one-track gravel road, ran by our house and went up a hill about a quarter mile away. An old trail, called a ridge road, also crossed the hill.

"We—my brother and sister and I—were up on the old ridge road picking huckleberries when we heard horses rushing down the trail toward us. They sounded like a big bunch of horses, very loud and fast.

"We thought we were going to get run down so we started screaming and running for home. But no horses appeared! The sound stopped before we got the few yards to the main road. Then we were really scared. I don't know what that sound was but we didn't go back there."

Casey Allen is another who shudders when she hears such tales, for she and her husband lived for a year in a Hell's Holler home where a troubled spirit occupied one of the rooms.

"The day we moved in," Casey said, "I wondered why the lady who had lived there before had left a rug in one of the bedrooms. Since we didn't have many things then, I was glad she did until I lifted the rug and saw the big, dark bloodstain that didn't look like it was over two days old.

"I had heard that a man had been killed years before in the house but because the blood looked so fresh I wondered what had been killed there recently. I called my husband and he figured a cat or something had been killed and the previous owners had just neglected to clean up the mess.

"I was pretty shook up but even more scared when I tried to clean up the stain. The blood wouldn't come off the floor no matter what I did. Finally I just decided the blood had soaked through the wood floor and would dry up eventually, so I covered up the stain with the rug and tried to forget about it.

"We tried to sleep in the room that first night and just about midnight the sound of dresser drawers opening and closing woke us up. The sound kept getting louder. It was too dark to see much but we were too scared to look anyway. We jumped out of bed and ran out of the room. The next morning I went in and moved the rug; the bloodstain looked fresh as ever. Once we stopped going into the room we didn't have any more problems.

"I don't know if anyone else moved into the house after we left. I hope it has been torn down by now because I wouldn't want anyone to have to go through what I did."

The day they moved out Casey took one last peek under the rug. The bloodstain was still fresh.

John Carr didn't see a ghost but he knows firsthand why one home in Hell's Holler was rumored to be haunted until the day it burned to the ground. On a Sunday evening in 1952 John walked his wife to church, his old yellow hunting dog trailing along. Not being partial to church, John left his wife to attend the meeting while he continued to stroll the dusty back roads.

"I came up all at once on a house where I didn't know the people and heard a woman scream, 'Oh, Lord! Oh, Lord!' I ran inside and there was an old woman about seventy years old carrying a lantern around and screaming. Two men were in the room, too. When I asked what was wrong, one of the men said his brother had cut himself and pointed to a bedroom. I ran in and there was a man lying in bed with his throat cut. Blood was running all over the bed and floor. A man sitting beside the bed was holding a bloody straight razor.

"The man looked up and smiled and I figured I had better run before he took after me. Sure enough, as soon as I was out the door I could hear him breathing behind me. The man was fatter than me and I ran as hard as I could but he just kept breathing right behind me.

"I finally thought I just can't go no more and figured I would turn and fight the man, razor and all. When I turned, though, all I saw was my old yellow dog, his sides heaving. It was him who had been trying to keep up with me and it was his breathing I heard.

"I never knew what happened at that house and I didn't ever go back to find out but I heard people say years later that the house was haunted until the day it burned down."

Today many of Hell's Holler's back roads have been paved and modern homes have replaced most of the dilapidated farmhouses—but the ghost stories still circulate. I am dubious about some of them. I find it hard to believe that a man with a wicked-looking Jack-o'-Lantern head roams the highways every Halloween. And I've heard the saga of a woman's bloody face appearing in the window when death is imminent in so many other areas that I am not convinced that it originated in Hell's Holler.

Nevertheless, something beyond human understanding is going on at Hell's Holler and personal experience has made me wiser. I no longer smile skeptically at anyone's halting story of a bewildering supernatural encounter.

The Ghost of Miss Mary
By Minerva Torbett

January 1985

*We were halfway down the stairs when I saw
Miss Mary's ghost coming up the steps toward us.*

Indian Springs Georgia State Park is the oldest state park
in the nation. Many beautiful homes and hotels have
been built here over the years but none is lovelier than
Rock Castle which was built before the Civil War.

In the early 1930s the castle was occupied by three
elderly heirs, Miss Carrie Collier, Miss Lou Collier, and
their niece, Miss Mary Cleveland. They maintained a
Children's Library in the left living room. The young people of the village were encouraged to check out books and
my friend Evelyn Archer and I made many visits to the
library. We liked to visit the elderly ladies because they
took us outside and explained a century plant and told us

why birds need a birdbath and then they always gave us a cookie or some sweets. We had learned to read before we entered first grade because of the Children's Library.

We were in third grade when a bad flu epidemic hit our town. Miss Mary, the niece, died within a week after becoming ill. The two aunts became sick within weeks of this loss; Miss Carrie was still up but Miss Lou, looking very pale, lay in bed.

Evelyn's mother called us in and told us we should go to see Miss Lou; she cautioned us not to stay too long and to be on our best behavior.

We were met at the front door of the Castle by the maid and sent on our way up the beautiful curving stairway to Miss Lou's bedroom. There we stood beside Miss Lou's bed holding her hands while we talked with Miss Carrie. In a short time we said our good-byes to both ladies and started down the dimming stairway.

We were halfway down the stairs when I saw Miss Mary coming up the steps toward us. I seemed to be able to see through her upper torso but there was no mistaking her face surrounded by the white pompadour of her hair. Evelyn and I rushed for the front door; we actually fell down the front steps, got up, and ran as fast as possible to the sandbar in the small creek that cuts through the park.

When we caught our breath, we agreed on exactly what we'd seen. No word passed between us from the time we started down the steps until we collapsed on the sand. Evelyn outran me to the spot.

Miss Lou died within a few days of our visit and Miss Carrie followed her shortly afterward. It was a sad time.

Today Rock Castle still stands, a shell, purchased by the Georgia State Park Division.

LOUISIANA

Ghosts of the Old New Orleans Jails
by Stan Reynolds

October 1992

A beautiful ghost haunted prisoners, causing them to attempt suicide!

Prisoners in old New Orleans had a lot more to worry about than just the loss of their freedom. As reported by the *New Orleans Daily Picyune* on January 23, 1882, there had been fourteen attempted suicides, most of them successful, in cell number 17 at the old Parish Prison.

Prisoners surviving the suicide attempts had babbled about seeing a beautiful, red-haired woman who walked into their cell. Smiling, she then tortured them so terribly that they tried to kill themselves to escape.

The continuing string of suicide attempts finally caused the prison warden to stop using cell number 17. The beautiful ghost then began haunting another cell on the same floor used for female prisoners. Within three months, six women confined to that cell had killed themselves. Several police officers at the prison reported seeing the striking apparition, who was so regal in bearing that they called her the "Redheaded Countess."

As later newspaper stories reported, there was even stronger testimony of the eerie incidents occurring at the old Ninth Precinct Station, which was commonly called the Carrolton jail.

In the hot New Orleans summer of 1899, Sergeant William Clifton, Commander of the Ninth Precinct, was visited at the jail office one evening by two men and a woman. As they talked, the woman leaned against the office wall and she was suddenly and violently spun out into the room. She returned to the wall and again attempted to lean on it. The same unseen force hurled her away. Not believing what they had just witnessed, Sergeant Clifton and the other two men then tried to lean on the wall, unsuccessfully. Each man, in turn, was forcefully pushed away by something they could not see, or understand. Puzzled, they stayed away from the wall.

A few nights later, the patrol wagon driver, Officer Dell, lay down on a sofa against the same wall. He said that the sofa suddenly moved to the center of the room and back. Disbelieving fellow police officers gathered in the room to watch as one of them lay down to test the sofa, which immediately tilted and bounced the skeptical policeman roughly on the floor.

After this incident, it was recalled that a man, arrested for murdering his wife and boiling her body in lye, had been beaten to death against that same wall by enraged policemen.

Following these strange incidents, the tough and thoroughly realistic group of officers assigned to the old jail was frightened by one spooky happening after another.

Mounted Officer Jules Aucoin entered the jail office in October 1899 and observed a framed portrait of Admiral Dewey revolving like a wheel on the wall. On closer examination, the portrait appeared perfectly normal, and was found to be hung securely. Another evening, a mirror and a framed portrait of General P. G. T. Beauregard both fell from the wall, crashing noisily to the floor in front of witnesses, with no discernible cause.

On another night, the sound of heavy footsteps, with one dragging foot, was heard in the jail corridor by Corporal Hyatt. No one was found in the corridor. Officers recalled the walking sound of a lame murderer, recently imprisoned, who had escaped. They later learned that on that same night they heard the ghostly footsteps, the escaped murderer had been found dead in Pennsylvania.

At midday the following July, the sergeant looked up to see two quadroon girls standing before his desk, smiling wickedly. Almost instantly, they disappeared in front of his eyes. The shaken sergeant recognized the images as those of the two women who had been hanged there for the crime of killing their lovers, whose livers they had carved out.

Cell number 3 in the Carrolton jail was the site of the most chilling chain of events. Each time that a prisoner was placed in the cell overnight, he would be found the next morning, beaten bloody and near death. Each victim, dazed and scared almost witless, repeated the same story. They all said that three ghostly men had come through the walls into the cell, and battled with each other, and with the mortal prisoner, throughout the night. Policemen recalled that three murderers had once been locked up together in cell number 3 overnight, and they had fought each other viciously all night long. The next morning, two were found dead, and the third died hours later.

Numerous transfer requests from policemen stationed there made staffing the Ninth Precinct difficult for many years.

The city of New Orleans finally had the decaying Carrolton Jail pulled down in 1937. Even then, as they razed the gallows in the jail courtyard, workmen and other witnesses reported seeing human shapes amid the clouds of dust. The grinning specters of every murderer who died there had returned to enjoy the final destruction of the grisly old prison.

My Friend, the Black Ghost Child

by Joan Briscoe

February 1975

No one but me believed in the existence of my friend Sarah until one afternoon when she showed me a whole shed full of human bones.

The most memorable friend of my childhood was invisible. I met her when my parents, Bill and Jenny Pevey, and I were living in an old house near Vivian in central Louisiana in the early 1930s. The house, built in the shape of the letter "L," stood silhouetted on a hill surrounded by barren fruit trees. A rutted dirt road led past to the hills and the forest where my father cut railroad ties for a meager living.

I was only six years old, but I knew from the beginning the house was haunted. Not only did it look spooky but I felt an eerie, clammy feeling, especially when I was alone. All of us were frightened. Mama and Papa soon noticed strange goings-on but discussed them guardedly.

The thing that bothered us most was the rear room that had been boarded up and put off limits to us. Our aged, uncommunicative landlord explained only that the room stored personal property. This would have been quite all right except that some of the things in storage there were noisy. A grandfather clock must have stood in the room against the thin wall of our bedroom. We never heard it tick, yet it chimed twelve times every midnight. And this chiming was followed by the sound of a rooster crowing from within the mysterious room. Otherwise we never saw or heard a trace of him.

I easily could have overlooked these things but there was one thing wrong with the house I could not forgive. I was an only child at that time and I was lonely and Papa often brought me pet cats but because of the atmosphere of the house, I couldn't keep one very long. Each kitten would depart leaving me with a newly broken heart.

Then one day in 1936 a little playmate arrived to help me forget my loneliness. She was a little black girl about my age and as pretty as could be. Sarah was friendly and mischievous, to my delight and to my parents' distress. And what's more—they couldn't see her!

Her invisibility to everyone except me delighted Sarah but often proved a detriment to me, for Mama and Papa would blame me for some of Sarah's antics they didn't find amusing. For instance, one day Sarah suggested we dip Mama's snuff. She insisted I fetch it from the mantel over the fireplace and bring it to our favorite hiding place. After one dip I wanted no more but Sarah loved it and plopped whole spoonfuls into her mouth, not even bothering to spit. It was amazing. Soon the bottle was almost empty and I didn't know how I was going to explain it to Mama. She and Papa got great pleasure out of their only luxury and I told Sarah that I was in for it. Sarah just shrugged her shoulders and suggested that I mix cocoa with what was left to fill up the bottle. After she left I did as she suggested. Sarah must have laughed and laughed over my being so naïve.

But there were fun times too. Sarah rarely came at night but one evening she visited when we were sitting around the large open fireplace. Mama was sewing and Papa was enjoying a last pipe before going to bed. I was snuggled at the end of the hearth watching the eerie shadows the fire cast against the unpainted plank walls when Sarah suddenly appeared right in front of my astonished eyes. As usual no one else could see her.

Immediately Sarah began running about the room amusing herself. Without warning she jumped impishly onto the back of Mama's rocking chair, giving her a quick jolt that caused her thread and scissors to slip from her lap onto the floor. When Mama stooped to pick them up Sarah pushed my cat's tail under the rocker. I reached down to pull the tail back but I was too late. Mama rocked back and the cat let out a spine-tingling meow. I have to admit it was quite a ruckus. Mama had spotted me reaching down and assumed I was at fault. She hit me so hard with the back of her hand I thought my jaw had cracked. I was so mad at Sarah I swore I'd never play with her again.

But Sarah wasn't through. She went over to tease Papa, who sat taking long drags on his pipe to calm his shattered nerves. Sarah reached down and scooped up a tiny dab of sawdust from the floor near the kindling box and flicked it over Papa's pipe. The fire in the pipe sputtered and Papa coughed. The pipe almost went out so Papa took a hefty puff to ventilate it. That was a mistake, I guess. I never saw so many sparks or heard such cussing in all my life. It was really a sight.

Sarah was bent over slapping her hands and legs and laughing like crazy. I got to slapping mine and laughing just the way she was. That was a mistake too. Papa got the notion I had something to do with the trick and sent me off to bed.

One day when Sarah came to play she wasn't in her usual happy mood. When I asked what was wrong she told me to come with her to a shed on the back of the property. I was forbidden to go there but as usual I followed Sarah's lead. I'll never forget what I saw there. It was enough to scare anyone right out of their wits—a whole shed full of bones!

After Sarah calmed me down we sat on a log and she explained that the bones belonged to early slaves who had lived on the place and worked for the first owner. He had been very mean and killed slaves when he was displeased with them. Rather than giving them a decent burial he had thrown their bodies into the shed in the back yard to decay.

Finally someone slew the slaveholder and relatives took over the house. The private things now stored in the sealed room had belonged to the original owner.

Sarah explained that her father had been killed by the mean man and her mother had died of grief. Sarah had died of exposure after her mother's death.

That was the last time I saw Sarah. We parted sadly. She didn't want to play that day and sent me to the woods where Mama and Papa were cutting wood. I wasn't my usual self that day either and my parents soon asked what was wrong. I couldn't hold back the truth even though I feared I might get a whipping for telling a lie. But they followed me back to the old shed and Papa peeked inside. "It's the truth!" he gasped.

That same day we packed our few belongings and left. On the way through town Papa stopped and asked the sheriff the truth about the old house and the bones. He told Papa the same story Sarah had told me. No one could explain how I had heard the story.

I started school later that year and was delighted with a new game I devised to make spelling tests more fun. I guessed the words and wrote them down on paper before the teacher called them, no matter how she mixed up the list. It was great fun; all I had to do was listen inside my head. But the teacher didn't think it was fun. She punished me for cheating although she couldn't explain how I managed it. Somehow I knew my mischievous friend Sarah was involved but didn't dare admit it.

Even now there are times when I "know" things before they happen. But I try to turn it off because I don't want to know. I just want to be normal and besides, I can't really trust that.

Noisy Phantom of the Louisiana Swamp

by Paul F. Serpas

October 1956

The weird whistling and barking approached our camp. I switched on the spotlight and saw—nothing.

It was coming closer. We could hear the leaves rustling close to the trail. Quietly I climbed into the overhanging branches of a young swamp tree. In one hand I carried a powerful navy spotlight, a war surplus job capable of lighting up the whole area.

Below me Charles Brand and two other friends were taking cover in and around the tents. We were ready to protect ourselves from whatever it was. As we waited in the pitch darkness, the whistling and barking came nearer.

Beads of perspiration trickled down the open neck of my shirt. The steaming heat of the swamp had not cooled, although it was almost 1:30 in the morning. In another minute, I thought, we would get a glimpse of the thing. It came relentlessly onward through the jungle-like foliage, directly toward our camp. I held the light in readiness.

We had started our camping trip early that summer morning. There were four of us: Emile, Archie, Charles, and I. It was only an overnight camping trip but one would have thought that we were going on safari into darkest Africa, judging from the large boxes of food and supplies we carried.

A friend volunteered to drive us a good part of the way or I doubt if we could have made it with most of the stuff. As it turned out, we managed to haul everything deep into the interior of the vast wooded area we had become so familiar with. We knew most of the trails leading in and out of this Louisiana swamp from our frequent weekend visits, when we fished or hunted wild birds and turtles. The huge palmetto plants and twisting vines that grow in the Louisiana swamplands are not unlike the tropical vegetation one finds in the African jungles. A hot sun beat down upon us as we walked along the winding footpaths. We carried two ten-gallon jugs filled with water for drinking and cooking. We had filled them at a trapper's cabin on the outskirts of the marsh and they were plenty heavy.

After a few hours we had found a suitable campsite where a small bush trail widened to about 15 square feet. The ground was high and dry and made an excellent overnight spot. It didn't take long for the four of us to set up camp. Emile and Charles started to get lunch while

Archie and I took off into the thicket to gather firewood. After lunch we went down to a little freshwater dock and tried our luck at fishing. Three small cats were all we got for our trouble.

Night was closing in when we finished dinner. Soon a heavy blanket of fog kicked up and swirled around our feet as we walked. Crickets and frogs began their songs, and the night took on an air of mystery. We spent most of the evening just sitting around the fire, exchanging friendly chatter. We discussed our plans for the following day, and not long afterward retired to our tents. Archie and Charles occupied one of the tents, Emile and I the other.

Smoldering embers were all that remained of the fire when Emile and I awoke simultaneously. The mosquitos were out in force, and the heavy netting we had hung over the doors didn't allow much of the night air to enter; consequently the heat added to our discomfort.

Both Emile and I lay there in the darkness, smoking and talking softly so as not to wake the others. Suddenly the silence was broken by the wailing and barking of what sounded like a large dog, some distance away.

It struck us as odd that a dog should be in the vicinity, but we dismissed it and continued our conversation. Then, from the same direction came another sound—of a man whistling! It was a tuneless sort of sing-song, weird to say the least. It startled us.

A few moments later we heard it again. This time closer than before. Again it came still nearer. Emile and I decided to wake the others.

We all sat together in my tent and listened. There it was—clear, unmistakable, and growing louder. Twigs and bushes began to rustle. Charles and Archie grabbed their guns. Emile took up his ax. I reached for the spot-light and made for the door.

Outside, the stillness of the night was almost a tangible thing. We spread out around the camp and I made my way over to the tree. All the while the sounds came closer. Now, I thought, it is within a few yards of us. I waited for a moment, making sure of the direction, then threw the switch on the big light. It was almost as if the sun had come out—but there was nothing there to be seen.

Thinking I had jumped the gun and missed him, I turned off the light. Darkness rushed in like water filling the hole.

My spine chilled and the hairs on the back of my neck began to tingle as once again the whistle pierced the night; this time from almost directly beneath me! Light swept over the entire area as I played the beam back and forth across the shadows, straining my eyes to see where the sounds were coming from. As far as I could see there was nothing!

We began to shout, to yell threats. There was no answer. Only the eerie sound of the ghostlike whistle and the rustling of the bushes broke the stillness—going away from us now. We sat quiet, unmoving.

The sounds did not stop but rather faded slowly into the distance, just as they had approached from the distance. It was almost as if a ghostly hunter and his dog had passed through our camp on their journey into eternity!

At last they were out of earshot. None of us could explain it then, nor can we now.

MARYLAND

Détente with a Ghost
By Arline Chase

June 1981

We knew the spirit hated us but we didn't know why until one day the situation came to a shattering climax.

In March 1964 our older son David was stricken with rheumatic fever and needed complete bed rest and plenty of peace and quiet. The mobile home in which we lived was compact and cozy but didn't have room for the kind of care he needed while we waited for construction of our house to be finished. My parents, Margaret and Arlington Adkins, who had just purchased a rambling ten-room house on Hudson Wharf Road near Cambridge, Maryland, solved our problem by asking us to stay with them until the carpenters could complete our place.

That's when the fun began!

Often as I climbed the circular front stairs, as narrow and steep as a mountain trail, I experienced a feeling of dread. As I went along the front hall I would feel as if I had passed someone there, catching a glimpse of him or her from the corner of my eye. But I never saw any clearly defined shape or anything I could definitely call a ghost. There was only the uncomfortable sense of something.

Still I was frightened. I tried to dismiss it as nerves. After all, I was worried about my son's illness and I was living in unfamiliar surroundings. Maybe these things were exciting my imagination. I didn't believe that for long, however.

The emotional climate in the house intensified into hostility and anger. I got the impression that it, whatever it was, resented our presence. It is hard to explain, but if you have ever entered a room in which a group of people have been quarreling violently, you may have felt the anger in the air even when no words were spoken while you were there. Most people are sensitive enough to pick up this unspoken message. Some people are more sensitive than others. I've learned from this experience that my own reception is better than average but not really exceptional.

One morning as I was having coffee in the sunny ell of the kitchen, my mother came down the back stairs to join me. "I made your bed while I was upstairs," she said casually. I was thunderstruck. I'd made that bed before coming downstairs that morning and as far as I could tell no one had been in the room in over three hours. I might have believed that I was mistaken but since having the four of us there made for so much extra housework, I tried to do as much of it as possible.

Later that day, when I went upstairs for some clean linen, I saw that the same bed had again been mussed. It did not look as if it had been slept in but as if someone had snatched at the covers and rumpled them as a child might do in a tantrum. I would have suspected my own children, except that their room was downstairs and one was too ill and the other too young to be able to climb the steps.

I began to be afraid to go upstairs alone. When I told my husband about it, he did not laugh as I had expected but confessed that he too often passed someone in the hall. Whenever he did, the hair on the back of his neck rose.

Neither of us ever noticed anything on the first floor. My husband had never felt the anger or hostility—what I called the "go away!" feeling. He claimed that whatever it was, it didn't frighten him. I agreed that most of what I was feeling could be imaginary. I tried my best to believe that. I wish I had known then what I have since learned: that hundreds of similar cases have been documented in this country in recent years.

One day a few weeks later as Mother and I were working in the kitchen, she suddenly asked me, "What makes you so angry with me?" Taken aback, I said I was not angry but she insisted she could feel the anger crackling in the air between us. Clearly she was getting the signals but mistaking the source. I wasn't angry but someone was! How could I tell her that her newly purchased house was haunted?

In the meantime the ghost's anger toward us intensified. Footsteps paced louder in the hall. Small objects—my hairbrush, my husband's keys—began to disappear from our bedroom. We always found them in the same place: inside the closed drawer of an empty bureau in one of the front bedrooms. Sometimes we heard loud rattling noises and always we had the feeling we were being watched even in our most intimate moments. I had to force myself to go upstairs and I would leave the light on in order to sleep. It took more courage than I possessed to go out into that hall and down the stairs to attend to the children when they called at night.

Then a few days later, as I started down the front stairs with a bundle of laundry, a hand pressed between my shoulder blades and shoved me headlong down those murderous twisting stairs.

Fortunately I caught the lintel over the stairwell and broke my fall, nearly tearing my arms from their sockets in the process. The laundry landed at the bottom with a soft plop. It was a long way down. I managed to swing myself back and dropped safely to the stairs below with a crash. As I sat there shaking all over, I could still feel the angry presence hovering over my left shoulder.

Mother ran in to see what all the noise was about and I told her I had stumbled. She looked at me strangely but returned to the kitchen when she saw that I was unhurt.

"Why?" I cried aloud. "Why do you hate me so? I haven't done anything to you." I knew she had deliberately pushed me down the stairs. She could have killed me! I wasn't even sure when it had become "she." Perhaps it was because the hand had not been cold and ghostly but perfectly ordinary, like that of someone standing behind me in line at the supermarket.

Suddenly the anger faded and a wave of sympathy and understanding washed over me. I felt a touch on my left shoulder, a gentle one. It seemed to say, "I'm sorry."

And then the presence was gone and I was back in the middle of an ordinary day. I made my way downstairs to wash the laundry, feed the baby, and play chess with my older son. But I knew that sooner or later I'd have to face up to what had happened and warn my parents about the ghost. What if she tried to hurt somebody else?

She never tried to hurt me again and while I often felt her presence, I was no longer so frightened. Strangely enough, she appeared to have become fond of me, following me from room to room as I did my upstairs chores. I got the impression that she was lonely and enjoyed my company, although she continued to be hostile toward my parents. She froze up if Mother entered a room where she was. At times she snooped around, listening at Mother's bedroom door. I wasn't certain how my parents would take it if I warned them. A repentant ghost is no more believable than any other kind.

When I did try to discuss the presence of the ghost, of course the whole thing was treated as a joke. When I tried to be serious no one except my husband would listen. My father flatly refused to discuss it and everyone considered it an amusing tale. But my husband backed me up. He told them that he, too, had felt something. His statement was met with a fresh round of laughter.

One morning in July, when we were having coffee, the next-door neighbor, Mrs. Meredith, stopped by. We asked her about the age of the house. She said her house and Mother's were about the same age and she had been living in hers ever since it was built nearly fifty years ago. She must have known my ghost! I decided to tell her about the phenomena I had experienced. Why not? By now I was used to ridicule.

Leaving out only the incident on the stairs, I told her the story and added that for some reason I felt as if the ghost were a woman about sixty-five or older, short and gray-haired with rimless glasses that had gold earpieces. The phantom paced up and down the front hall and was angry. Sometimes the footsteps were clearly audible. She disliked the people in my mother's bedroom although I did not feel the resentment applied so much to Mother and Dad as to the people who had occupied the room in her lifetime. She never went into that room, which was in the ell, although she sometimes followed me into my room which was adjacent to it. Her main interests were the front bedrooms, hall, and stairs.

I said she was a possessive person who felt that the house still belonged to her. While she tolerated Mother, who didn't sleep in her part of the house, she resented us much more actively because we were occupying her space.

Having gotten it all out at last, I felt better, although Mrs. Meredith had warned me at the outset that she didn't believe in anything supernatural. Nonetheless she exclaimed, "I know who that is! That's Bertha Sherman!"

Mrs. Meredith told us that "Miss Bertha" had rented the house soon after it was built and lived there many years. When her growing family got too large for the dwelling, the ell had been added. As the years passed and her family grew up and left home, the rent became less profitable to the owner and he decided to sell. He offered the house first to the Shermans, who could not afford to buy it, and then sold it to another couple who hoped to use it for a retirement home.

The new owners felt bad about Mr. and Mrs. Sherman and hated to force them out of the house they had lived in for over twenty-five years. So they agreed to rent them the front half of the house keeping only the ell for their own use on the weekends. The agreement was that the Shermans could stay at least until the new owners retired. Mrs. Sherman, who resented the new people bitterly, often made noises in her part of the house to annoy them. They slept in the bedroom now occupied by my parents.

The Shermans continued to live in the house until Mrs. Sherman's death from cancer in 1931. Although they spent a lot of money on improvements, the new owners were never satisfied and the house was sold again within six months of their moving into full-time occupancy. Mrs. Meredith confirmed that it had changed hands often. No owner seemed to stay more than a year and rental tenants left even more quickly.

I had known none of this history of the house when we went there. I had never heard of Bertha Sherman or her problems. Yet somehow I knew of them. Just how I knew, I'm still not sure. At least every perception I'd had conformed perfectly with the facts Mrs. Meredith gave us about her erstwhile neighbor, even to the physical description and the glasses she wore.

The front bedroom where we usually found the missing objects had been her bedroom and some of her furniture, including the bureau, was still in the house! She had been in the habit of pacing up and down the upstairs front hall whenever she was upset. Possessed of a legendary temper, she sometimes screamed so loudly at her landlords that her words could be heard next door. How well I knew that temper! I could still feel that hand between my shoulder blades.

People who thought the ghost was a figment of my imagination were surprised that she didn't disappear when we moved into our own home. But "Miss Bertha" is still there. Others have heard her in the front hall and on the stairs. She slams doors and opens them too, especially when someone is undressing. She even bounced up and down on a bed while one of Mother's house guests was trying to sleep.

Well, it isn't every ghost who develops such a sense of humor. And although she has become something of a practical joker, at least most of the anger and malevolence have disappeared. She seems more receptive to house guests these days, even to the point of tucking in the children's covers when they visit for an occasional weekend. And why shouldn't she? She's had plenty of practice. She raised five children of her own in her house.

Our Friendly Peg-Legged Poltergeist

By Gene Shumate

July 1978

*We now know ghosts are not all bad, for Siegfried
(as we called him) did no real harm—although he
scared the bejeebers out of us.*

Friends and relatives didn't believe us at first—now they
do. A poltergeist or some otherworldly force shared our
Tudor-style home in Silver Spring, Maryland, for about
eleven years. The ghostly prankster scared the bejeebers
out of us for a while but when he didn't do any real harm
we began to realize that all ghosts are not bad. We hung
on him (or was it her?) the good old northern name
Siegfried, for whenever he was near the air was colder
than usual.

Skeptical at first, we paid little attention to the noises
in the basement at night. After all, a fifty-year-old house
should be allowed to settle and creak in peace. But we
had to rule out this explanation when Siegfried began to
groan and whistle in long, low tones.

Early on (in 1966 or 1967) my wife Grace was doing
the laundry in the basement and three different lights
were burning. One after another they went out, leaving
her in total darkness. When I went down with a flashlight
I found the bulbs had not burned out; somehow they had
been loosened in their sockets. We blamed Siegfried—and
we also blamed him for articles that turned up missing,
doors that opened by themselves, and the bat that got
into our daughter Gretchen's bedroom.

One Sunday afternoon in the winter of 1968-1969,
Grace's sister, Evaleen Watts, her three children, Grace,
and I were gathered around the dining room table when
all of us heard an even thump, thump, thump—like something soft but heavy rhythmically hitting the asphalt tile
floor in the basement. Our visitor paled. Bravely locking
hands, we went below to investigate.

I had been using a power saw earlier in the day and
the floor was covered with fine sawdust. Clearly visible in
the dust were footprints leading from the work area to an
unused room. Strangest of all, the prints had been made
by a bare right foot, too large for anyone in our house,
and a scuff mark where a left foot should have been. The
kids spied the prints first, shrieked in unison, and have
not returned to the basement to this very day.

In the old days when our home was built the technol-
ogy to shear off rock which lay in the way of the foundation was unknown. Bricklayers simply worked up and

around the large boulders. When laying our foundation they left a boulder that stretches almost the length of the house and rises eight feet above the basement floor. Long ago the unsightly rock had been enclosed in a special room with entrances at each end where I stored lumber and lawn furniture.

With the kids screaming and crying upstairs, we adults followed the footprints to one of the doors of the "rock room." We found it unlocked and standing open, although I always kept it locked. Inside the room, to our amazement, we found a pile of objects that had been missing for years—among them, a cookout brazier and a heavy bust of George Washington. Also among the clutter we found an old painting of a Victorian woman, tight-lipped and proper. We had never seen it before.

In the fall of 1971 our daughter Gretchen Jolles and her husband Jeff came to stay with us while awaiting completion of their home in Gaithersburg, Maryland. Despite the episode of the bat in her bedroom before she married, we had never told her about Siegfried.

"Dad," she said to me one day, "every time I'm downstairs near the rock room I feel a strange tugging. It feels like there's a big magnet in that rock room. Funny, isn't it?" I laughed and shrugged it off.

Two nights later we were all awakened by an intermittent whirring sound in the basement. Once again we went down in a group to look around. Someone—I'm convinced it was that rascal Siegfried—had opened Gretchen's sewing machine, plugged it in, and set it to stitching. This happened more than once before Gretchen and Jeff moved out.

Our outer basement door has five locks on it including a deadman bolt, which requires a key to open whether from inside or out. We rarely open the door—maybe twice a year to clean the drain gutter in the areaway. But twice in the winter of 1974 we felt an icy draft while we were having breakfast. Both times we found that basement door standing wide open with no sign of forced entry—and the two keys to the deadbolt lock were safely upstairs on a key chain. Since then our dog, an alert schnauzer who once loved to romp in the basement, refuses to go down there alone. But he often bristles and scratches on the door to the basement stairway; the heavy oak door is a mass of scars.

Lately my brother-in-law Joe Berry has been living on the second floor of our house. At the base of the staircase leading to his rooms there's a door with an old-fashioned lock, the kind that can be opened by any of the other door keys. However, we keep all of our door keys on the molding over the doors so that our grandchildren can't mischievously or accidentally lock them.

Joe runs a seafood restaurant, which is open late into the night, so he sleeps in every morning. One afternoon he awakened and although he was alone in the house he found himself locked in. Joe was tying sheets together so that he could lower himself out the window when he spied the mailman. Joe yelled to him for help and tossed out his front door key. The postman came in and opened the staircase door—using the key that dangled mysteriously from the keyhole.

More recently someone gave us a book from the Edgar Cayce Foundation in Virginia Beach, Virginia. The unopened package was tossed on a bed while Grace and I went out. On our return we found the book unwrapped and neatly opened to a chapter dealing with poltergeists.

Since then Siegfried hasn't been around. Maybe he moved on because we weren't afraid of him anymore and he wasn't having any fun. We truly miss him. How does one ask a friendly ghost to come home? All is forgiven.

The Pottery Went A-Dancing

By Harlan Wilson

June 1960

A poltergeist apparently was calling the tune when objects in this Baltimore home did the rock-'n-roll.

The mystery began about 11 A.M. on Thursday, January 14. Fifteen miniature pottery pitchers had been sitting on the shelf in the dining room. For no apparent reason they all exploded simultaneously.

For the next several days the events in the house at 1448 Meridene Drive, Baltimore, Maryland, defied rational explanation.

They began with a characteristic action by the family's dog, Kristi. Mrs. Theodore C. Pauls, who lives in the home with her husband, her seventeen-year-old son Ted, and her parents, Mr. and Mrs. Edgar G. Jones, described how the dog behaved.

"Kristi would begin to claw at us and then we would know something was going to happen. But we don't really know why."

The events that Kristi foretold were the phenomena that are typically attributed to poltergeists—also called "noisy ghosts" and "split-off portions of the psyche."

A flower pot jumped from a shelf in the dining room through a window and landed on the windowsill outside. A sugar bowl leaped about four feet to dump its contents in the candle holders of the chandelier.

In the living room, a brass incense burner left its place on a bookshelf and landed about six feet away. In the kitchen a plant jumped out of its holder on a wall and fell onto the table below.

Iced tea glasses toppled off a shelf. Ashtrays dropped to the floor from the top of the refrigerator. A bag of manure in the basement fell to the floor. A can of soup fell from a shelf. Wall pictures smashed to the floor.

Mrs. Pauls took some valuable miniature pottery pieces off the shelves in her bedroom and placed them on top of her bed. They were smashed right there.

"I tell you, it's got us crazy. We're scared to death," Mrs. Jones declared. "I hope someone can do something for us. We're all going to be sick."

Mr. Jones observed that the phenomena "follow us wherever we go. We hear the crashes but we've never been around when they happen."

Baltimore newspaper reporters, more sophisticated than most, immediately concluded that if the events were happening in the Jones-Pauls home as described, they were probably due to "poltergeist" phenomena.

They reported additional damage in the home. Seven bottles of soft drinks exploded in the basement; a can of sauerkraut fell off a shelf and hit Mr. Jones on the head; a small table fell down the stairs; a stack of kindling wood exploded.

Since the Baltimore reporters have heard about psychic phenomena, they began to look about for an agent who might be responsible for poltergeist-caused occurrences. The *Baltimore Evening Sun* quoted Professor William Henry Salter, the famed psychical researcher, to the effect that "poltergeist cases show a degree of uniformity which is remarkable. The agent is often a girl, less often a boy, rarely an adult." They also mentioned Professor Salter's view that when investigators appear on the scene the manifestations usually stop.

But a red-hot poltergeist case doesn't happen every day and reporters converged on the house. Some came from Washington and some from even farther afield.

The agent appeared obvious to them. It was probably seventeen-year-old Theodore C. Pauls, they decided. They observed that Ted "stays in the house most of the time" and seems interested in science fiction.

Ernest B. Thurgurson of the *Baltimore Sun* declared in a by-lined story that Ted was the only completely undisturbed occupant of the house.

"Ted sat in his rocker in front of the TV set, just listening, not talking, his arms crossed across his chest, a stack of science fiction books alongside his feet. He rocked, and rocked, and rocked," Thurgurson wrote.

While other members of the family talked excitedly Ted just sat there. All kinds of theories were proposed. Someone asked Ted if he had any ideas.

"No," he said.

Ted was asked if, as a science fiction fan, he thought what was happening in the house would make a good science fiction story.

"No," he said.

A reporter mentioned to Ted that phenomena like these do happen in households where there is an adolescent around to create unused psychic energy.

No comment.

Thurgurson reported that Ted did not appear to object to the word "adolescent." However, his rocking speeded up.

It turns out that Ted has been such a devoted science fiction fan that he has edited his own fan magazine—of the type called "fanzines" by science fiction addicts. In one of his fan magazines, called *Fanjack 2*, Ted mentioned some of the books be reads, including *Mad Magazine*; *Dr. Jekyll and Mr. Hyde*; *Fire Prevention*; *Witchcraft in America*; *The Report on Unidentified Flying Objects*; and Jack Kerouac's *The Beat Generation*.

One reporter finally asked Ted directly, "You are doing all this, aren't you, Ted?"

"No, sir," said Ted.

The reporters seemed to feel that the existence of poltergeist phenomena in a house where a young boy was both a science fiction fan, a UFO fan, and had an interest in psychic phenomena was too much of a coincidence.

Ted's reply to this line of inquiry was, "But I'm not doing it, I tell you. Besides, it would be a whole lot worse if I had a chemistry set down there in the basement. blowing up a lot of things, wouldn't it?"

Later on, the boy issued a more formal explanation for his keeping his lip buttoned. Travis Kidd and Michael Naver, writing in the *Evening Sun* on Thursday, January 21, quoted Ted as follows:

"The explanation...for my lack of comment on the strange happenings...does not come from my being passive toward the mess but rather from being introverted. I just cannot speak at length with people whom I have not been acquainted with for some time."

Mrs. Jones' maid, Mrs. Elizabeth Taylor, stated that she watched a cardboard shoe box rise from a bed and then fall on some potted violets, crushing the leaves. This appears to be the one instance in which there was an actual eyewitness to the phenomena.

Meanwhile, as is usual in such cases, all manner of substitute theories were proposed.

One man, a moving-van driver who described himself as a "ghost neutralizer," began to pray around the rooms in such a loud voice that he was ejected. He phoned later to say that he was lighting candles and continuing prayer to "purify" the house.

Stanley P. Greenfield, who runs a television and radio repair shop, announced that the culprit is really a big storm drain that runs behind the Jones house. He said that the pipe acted like a resonator, occasionally hitting just the right pitch to make things bounce or shatter. If so, the dog Kristi is the only one who hears it.

It was also variously proposed that the phenomena were caused by mysterious radio waves, an underground stream, a magnetic field set up by the electrical wiring, and just plain ghosts.

Douglas Dean, a researcher for the Parapsychology Foundation, arrived to gather data and take photographs. A few days later, Dr. Nandor Fodor, a New York psychoanalyst and psychic investigator (and FATE author) also appeared on the scene.

Whatever the conclusions may be, it will take some tall explaining to give an answer to such events as these, all of which occurred in the home within a half hour:

(1) The dining room chandelier went crazy; (2) a basement lamp toppled over; (3) an artificial Christmas tree took a two-foot free flight; (4) mop handles fell off the wall; (5) an ash tray exploded; (6) another ash tray cracked; (7) a stack of coasters flew around the room; (8) a flower pot cracked.

Things were really jumping around the Jones home, but explanations, as in most poltergeist cases, remained indeterminate, confused, and there "was always that element of doubt."

SOUTH
CAROLINA

The Ghost of Mr. Cheatham

By Raymond B. Padgett

May 1979

When I spoke the ghostly typing sound suddenly stopped and an ominous silence fell.

As a boy I responded to stories of ghostly encounters with translucent bravado and outward derision. Yet fear and dread clutched my spirit when older people spoke of the ghost of a murdered man trying to attract attention by dragging chains through the halls of a farmhouse and pulling the covers from occupied beds. Great-aunt Anne Ramsey had invisible dog friends and was fascinatingly convincing when she petted them and talked to them. By the time I was eight years old I was

133

thoroughly conditioned for my own encounter with the ghost of the Old Cheatham Place, where we lived for several months in 1924.

The Cheatham Place was a rambling fourteen-room frame house situated in a fifty-acre grove amid shrubbery so overgrown it concealed the house from passersby on the streets of Edgefield, South Carolina. It was the ancestral home of the *Edgefield Chronicle* editor, Lewis Wigfall Cheatham, who occupied it and did most of his work there until the demise of the paper in the early 1920s and his own death a few months before we moved in.

The people of Edgefield talked a lot about the ghosts in the Cheatham house and I heard of no one whose mind was closed to the possibility. It was a natural haunt for spooks. Dad told me not to panic if I met the ghost.

"He will only be trying to communicate something of importance," Dad said. "There is no record of a ghost ever hurting anyone. I never saw one but always wished I could."

My mother told me just to act natural and ask the ghost, "What in the name of the Lord do you want?" They are supposed to answer when asked in that exact manner.

Many strange noises could be heard in the old Cheatham house during quiet afternoons when Dad was at work and Mother was attending club meetings. Moans and creaks and slamming blinds kept the place alive. Sometimes there were sounds approximating heavy human footsteps, louder than the scuffling of flying squirrels and raccoons in the loft, louder even than the deafening hammering of woodpeckers. I nurtured my weakening determination to hold my ground but finally rationalized that ghosts cannot climb trees.

After that comforting decision most of my solitary hours were spent in the crotch of a giant magnolia tree. However, hungry after school, eventually I would have to enter the kitchen to get the lunch Mother always left on low heat. (She was a seamstress, practical nurse, and devout church worker, and when she was fitting dresses or caring for the sick, I suppose she thought that a manchild of hers, properly provided with food, could darned well take care of himself.)

The kitchen was a recent addition with two interior windows looking into the half of the house we didn't use, where cobwebs covered the library, shrouding antique furniture, office equipment, type galleys, an ancient square piano, (with its own medley of sounds when the temperature changed) and a typewriter. I ate at a table placed beneath these windows. Seated there one quiet afternoon, I encountered the ghost of the Old Cheatham Place. There was no doubt about it.

Suddenly the sound of a typewriter shattered the silence. I know now that the machine was handled with the professional rhythm of an expert and the invisible typist maintained a steady seventy-five words per minute. I could hear the clunk of the returning carriage. Remembering Mother's instructions, I jumped up and shouted, "What in the name of the Lord do you want?"

The sound of typing immediately gave way to an ominous silence and the ghost did not answer. I was already out of range anyway, with empty stomach and pounding heart, safe in the crotch of my magnolia tree.

Later, when I told my father what Mister Cheatham's ghost was up to, he said, "It was windy today. You just heard two beams rubbing together or something like that. Settle down and forget about it."

But I could not forget. I became almost hysterical as I thought about that clattering typewriter. Probably feeling harassed, Dad was somewhat rough when he grasped my shoulder, led me to the double doors opening into the storage area, unlocked them, and gave me a conducted tour by flashlight.

"See?" Dad said. "There's his typewriter up there on the shelf, covered with half an inch of dust. Surely if he wanted to type he would move the typewriter to this table. You're just imagining things and I want you to get a hold of yourself."

During the long spring afternoons for months after that I could comfort myself with a visual memory of the dust-covered typewriter while I ate my lunch and listened to an entire edition of the defunct *Edgefield Chronicle* in the clattering throes of creation. I wondered how beams rubbing together could make that sound: I accused my imagination of playing dirty tricks; I prickled all over and my hair stood erect; and in the end I became absolutely certain that I was living in the same house with a ghost.

A cat confirmed the occult presence in terms I could not ignore. On the day of our joint encounter, my huge yellow-brindle tomcat was sitting in a chair beside me when the typewriter started to clatter. Springing to emergency alert, Old Yellow stood his tail, his hair, and his ears at strict attention, paused only a split second, then literally flew into the screen door with enough force to rip the wire and escape. His explosive action robbed me of all composure and I followed him at equal speed, finishing the destruction of the door.

From that day forward I adamantly refused to enter the Old Cheatham Place unless both my parents were with me. Even with their dubious protection I kept my ears and running gear at the alert. I did not care what in the name of the Lord Mr. Cheatham's ghost wanted. All I wanted was for him to keep his distance. My parents resolved the matter by moving into another temporary home until our new house across town was completed.

There could be no doubt that a ghost frequented the Old Cheatham Place. Old Yellow made that clear.

The Plantation's Loving Ghost

By Ann Jensen

June 1965

The tiny old lady had a sentimental mission that kept her high heels tapping about the house late at night.

Two dear friends of mine own one of the loveliest plantations in the Carolinas. The house was built before the Civil War by Bert's great-grandparents. The first time I visited there I expected it to be beautiful but I was unprepared for the feeling of warmth and love that poured from the very soul of the well-preserved mansion.

Helen Houston and I arrived at dinner time. Although we were later than they expected us to be, we were greeted warmly. We ate our delicious dinner with heirloom silver, off of priceless antique plates. Our water goblets were old Baccarat. After dinner we retired to the front parlor and spent the evening with neighbors who came in to meet us.

It was midnight before the last good-byes were said. My host and hostess took us up the long stairway and down a wide hall to separate rooms. In my room Bert turned on the very modern electric lights that barbed the beautiful room in a soft glow. It was a large room with a marble fireplace, gigantic canopied bed and matching chests, dressers and chairs.

"It's beautiful," I whispered, as if I were in a cathedral.

Bert and Adeline were pleased with my delight in their home. They said so and wished me goodnight.

Tired from the long day's drive, I lost no time in getting ready for bed. The covers were turned back; a quilt of unusual design covered the sheets. It was made of white squares on which had been appliquéed circles of moss roses. I studied the tiny quilting stitches and wondered about the person who created this work. She's an artist, that's for sure, I concluded.

I climbed on the stool that helped me to get into the high bed. I put out the light and must have gone to sleep immediately.

I was awakened after what seemed like hours by the tap-tap-click-click of high heels on the polished staircase. I sat up in bed. "That's not Adeline," I thought. "She had on flats." Now the steps came down the hall—light, quick steps. They were coming to my door. I sat waiting, expecting a knock, but nothing happened. Turning on the bedside lamp, I looked at my watch. It was only 1:30. I turned the light off.

"Maybe it's just squirrels on the roof," I mumbled to myself sleepily. I settled back on my pillow and dozed off.

"Tap-tap-click-click" again up the stairs and straight to my room came the staccato sound of clicking heels. Wide awake now, I turned on the light. "Someone's in trouble," I murmured as I climbed from the bed and reached for my robe. The quick, light footsteps were going back to the staircase. Rushing to the door I pulled it open.

There at the head of the stairs stood a tiny, fragile lady about seventy years old. She held a white porcelain lamp in her left hand, high enough so that it illuminated her face there in the darkness of the hall. She had a sweet, patient face crowned by white curls that gleamed in the glow of the lamp. "She wears those piled-tip curls and high heels to make herself taller," I smiled with a rush of tenderness at her girlish vanity.

"Is something wrong; can I help?" I asked.

Smiling, she shook her head, waved her right hand in a gay little salute and raced down the stairs. "I couldn't make it half that fast," I thought as I watched her go with admiring astonishment.

It was then I saw the real beauty of her lamp. Around its porcelain surface were entwined little pink roses just like the quilt. Getting back into bed, I looked at my watch. It now read 2:30. 1 put out the light and slept.

Adeline and Helen and I were eating breakfast when Bert came in from a tour of his fields. He poured himself coffee and sat down with us.

"How'd you sleep?" He asked the routine question of a perfect host. "Oh, just fine." My answer also was given without thought. Then I remembered the beautiful lady on the stairs. "But, Bert, who is the lovely little lady—

white hair, high in curls here—like so," I was busy demonstrating, "and the highest heels."

Adeline clattered her coffee cup. I looked at her and she was staring at me as though I'd lost my mind.

"Really, Adeline," I said, "she woke me up twice last night. The second time I asked her if I could help her and she just smiled and waved to me."

I looked at Bert. He was busy trying to dig a cigarette out of a pack. His hand trembled. I took a deep breath. I knew I'd hurt them in some way. Probably it was a flighty relative who made her home with them. What could I say?

"What did she look like and how old was she?" Bert asked and struck a match for his cigarette.

"And what did she have on?" Adeline seemed less tense.

"In her seventies, I'd say. That's why I couldn't believe the high heels. She was very beautiful—wore a white blouse and dark skirt." I smiled.

"Honey, it was Grandma." Bert said gently. "High heels and all. She never would wear any other kind."

"You were in her room. She moved into it after Grandpa died," Adeline explained, "and we moved downstairs into their suite."

Bert got up and poured himself another cup of coffee.

"I'd like to meet her. She was probably upset because you put me in her room." I wanted so much to put them at ease about their aging relative.

"Grandma died twenty years ago." Bert sat down and reached for the sugar bowl.

I'd seen, heard, and known about the supernatural all my life, but Grandma wasn't a ghost. Grandma was a warm, living doll. "No," I cried out in protest, "No, I saw her—swift little feet in high heels, the sheen of her white curls in the glow of that lamp—no!"

They looked at me and then I knew that they knew what I had seen.

"She keeps coming back. We wonder if she wants to tell us something." Bert's face was full of concern, and I knew he wanted to talk about it.

"I try to take the same care of her things as she did, but," Adeline sighed, twisting a diamond solitaire on her finger, "this was hers, too. She gave it to me just before she left."

"And didn't leave at all," Bert sighed too.

"You don't like for her to visit?" I asked.

"Lord, yes, if that's what it is; but we have the feeling she wants us to do something." He looked puzzled.

I remembered the smile Grandma gave me, the wave of her hand. She wasn't sad at all and she shook her head when I asked if she wanted help.

"Do you ever speak to her?" I asked.

Both of them jumped.

"Of course not," Adeline answered.

"But she was warm and loving? No house could feel like this one does without a tremendous amount of love having lived here."

"Well, of course, and we loved her, too." Adeline fingered her napkin.

"We still love her and miss her," Bert added.

"Why don't you tell her so the next time you see her?" They didn't answer my question.

"It won't hurt anything," I kept persuading until they agreed to try talking to Grandma.

Afterwards Bert took Helen and me into his office to see pictures of his prize cattle and the blue ribbons they had won. One wall was given over to these trophies. It was a pleasant room. Over his desk he had grouped pictures of his children, grandchildren, and other members of the family. There in the center of all of them was a lovely smiling face with piled-up curls.

"Grandma," I said, pointing to it.

Bert smiled. We turned to go and then I saw it—Grandma's lamp—alone on a marble-top table, each moss rose in place.

"The lamp, with the same moss roses as the quilt; this is the lamp I saw, Bert."

"Yes, I know. Grandma made the quilt to match it."

That night I slept without disturbance. The next morning Adeline and Bert were at the breakfast table. They jumped up as I came in. Adeline poured orange juice and Bert filled my coffee cup. Both of them were in high spirits.

"Did you see Grandma last night?" Adeline asked.

"No, I'm sorry, I didn't." I shook my head.

"Well, we did—and we spoke to her like you said." Adeline's eyes filled with tears. "I'm so happy," she sniffed.

"I said to her 'Grandma, we love you' and you know what?" Bert was filled with wonder as he said this, and his face shone with the joy of it all.

"What?" I asked.

"Grandma smiled at both of us. Then she was gone."

They spoke again of Grandma's loving kindness, her ability, and most of all, her patience.

"Her patience—just think, she's been waiting around all these years just to hear us speak to her." Bert's eyes glowed. "There's nothing like it, just nothing like it—her love would not let her go until we knew she still lived."

Haunted House in
South Carolina
By Lee R. Gandee

April 1961

Hearing noises by agencies that could not be seen was bad enough—but seeing what walked across the kitchen was even worse.

Some old houses seem benevolent, so that one senses an unspoken welcome on entering. Some old houses seem secretive and sly. An occasional old house seems permeated with unspeakable memories.

There is a house such as the latter in Camden, South Carolina, at 116 Mill Street. It's been considered haunted for well over a century. Consequently during much of this time it has stood vacant, with owls and bats in its gloomy attic and only shadows in its rooms.

It is a mysterious place; no one knows when or by whom it was built, what happened in it, when or why it became haunted. The oldest plans of Camden Town show it as standing and tradition says that from 1820-1825, when a primary school was held in it by day, it was already an old house. The late Miss Kennedy, a very aged woman, whose grandmother attended this little school, remarked that children were afraid to remain late there, so apparently it had an evil reputation even then. And persons then alive may have known its tragedy. At that time, a forest stood between it and the village, and children sometimes saw deer and fawns on the path leading to the isolated house.

Usually one can determine the approximate age of an old house by its architecture. In Camden it is fairly safe to date a house as ten years to a generation later than similar examples of known age on the coast, in Charleston or Georgetown. By this rule, the building should date within ten years of 1780, for its great room is pure Georgian, typical of the middle half of the eighteenth century. Its craftsmanship suggests that slave-artisans trained in Charleston built it. Its quality is underwritten by the fact that one of the Du Pont family tried to buy the woodwork to decorate her own mansion.

The style of the house is part of its mystery. Everything indicates that the house was part of a larger plan that never was carried out. One can visualize the great room joined by a hall to a matching room and provided with a second story. The great, squat, massive chimney seems built to support a second flue, and the large room—

twenty feet long and almost as wide—is out of all proportion to the rest of the house. Had the seemingly intended plan been completed, the finished structure would have been a balanced, Georgian mansion of some importance. It was fairly common for young couples to begin a house in this manner, adding space as growing families and increased means made it desirable. This house was begun by a man of means and refined taste; that he did not complete it suggests that his life in Camden—and perhaps on earth—ended prematurely and tragically.

The contrast between the fine big room, rich with dentilwork and cornice moldings, dado, and wainscotted end wall, and the ramshackle, nondescript little rooms that were added later suggests that the house passed into the hands of someone of a lower class who had neither means nor taste.

Before the Civil War the forest was cleared away and fields were plowed where the trees had been. At that time, crops were planted up to the walls of the old house and it was used to store grain and cotton. The Kennedy family farmed the land during that period. Subsequently the house was owned for a long time by the Zorn family, and later by a Mr. Guy. After standing vacant for twenty years or more it was bought by a Mr. Wilson.

Mr. Wilson owned the property when I lived in Camden and became familiar with it in 1956. When he bought the house the glass was out of the windows, the weatherboarding was decayed, but the frame was sound. At the time when Mr. Wilson bought it, houses of any description were not plentiful in Camden. It was a fine lot and the price was ridiculously low—$1,500! He began an ambitious renovation. He put on a good roof, covered the rotting weatherboards with imitation brick siding, shored up the sagging porches, painted the interior, installed electric wiring and running water. Perhaps he even felt pleased with his bargain—for a little while.

When word got out that he had bought the old house, Wilson began to receive visits from interested people. Antiquarians came to dicker for the old trammels from the kitchen fireplace, the fine hinges, and other ironwork, and when he discovered an antique broad ax sealed in the kitchen wall, its ancient appearance caused a stir. A collapsed barn, supposedly as old as the house, lay at the back of the lot.

In clearing away this debris, Mr. Wilson found a rusted flintlock rifle concealed beneath what had been the barn floor. This also caused speculation and curiosity. Finally the venerable Miss Kennedy came and showed him where her grandfather had lost a fine horse. It had plunged forty feet through rotten logs into a concealed well and broken its neck and almost dragged valuable slaves into the well with it. Miss Kennedy said her grandfather had inquired and found out that, long before, the well had become foul, had been covered over and forgotten.

In telling me of the broad ax, Mr. Wilson said: "You know, it was one of them old kind with a wide, flat blade that they used to hew out timbers. It was as keen as a razor, and bright except where there was a rust stain on it. Funny thing, that stain! It had eaten into the steel, and you could trace splatters on it, and where something bad run on the blade, like where you kill chickens with an ax and don't wipe it off—that's how it appeared to me; and they left it like that and nailed it up behind the boards in the kitchen wall."

However, he did not give the ax, the rifle, and the old well much thought until after he had lived in the house for some time. He built a shack in the back yard and planted a garden in the rich ground where the barn had been. He rented the little house to an elderly woman, who also planted part of the garden. For months everything was tranquil.

Then one day as he was hoeing his cabbages Wilson noticed dust spurt up at his feet. He paused and looked, thinking that someone had thrown a rock, but there was no one in sight. Nevertheless, dust was puffing up as if a shower of stones or brickbats was striking the ground all about the garden. He was deeply puzzled by this, but said nothing for fear of alarming his eighty-year-old tenant, whose ten dollars a month was very welcome. For a time the puffs of dust flew up almost every time he worked in the garden. He mentioned it to his mother who was the only other member of the household, but she could not explain it any better than he.

Then one day they heard the old woman cry out and hurried to see what was the matter. They found her trying desperately to open the garden gate, which was secured by a stiff wire hooked over a nail. She could not undo it and as they watched, "she flopped down and wriggled under the wire fence like a sow," Mr. Wilson said. She was completely beside herself, babbling about brickbats flying through the air all around her, and asking what a poor helpless old woman was to do when things struck her that she could not see! She called her children forthwith, and the little house was cleared of her belongings before sundown.

Soon after this, as Wilson was working in the garden trying to ignore the puffs of dust rising around him, he and his mother heard what they thought was a shot. Each ran to see about the other. Mrs. Wilson rounded the corner of the house as her son came from the garden into the yard. They asked each other what the noise was and, as they stood talking, something passed by them. What passed was invisible to them.

Mr. Wilson said, "That thing—God knows what it could have been—you could feel it was there, and it made a noise like wasps when you get them mad and they start buzzing on the nest. It went right past our faces. It scared us, for it was blazing hot. It felt like somebody had passed a smoothing iron right in front of your face, slow like."

"Did you see anything?" I asked him.

"No, not then," he considered. "No; that hot thing can't be seen. It just buzzes, and we found out that you only hear and feel it when you hear the noise like a rifle shot. I recollect one time Mother and me was in the big room and heard the shot noise outside, and I stepped to the door to look out. It passed through the room then, and out through the door right past me, hot enough to singe you!"

I asked what other noises they had heard and what other phenomena the Wilsons had observed. The three of us were sitting in the large room. This room also contained the Wilsons' beds.

"You hear footsteps," Wilson said tensely, "and sometimes you hear like two men arguing. That gets pretty loud, but you can't make out what they say. Then once we heard walking in the back bedroom, and the noise of somebody throwing down an armload of firewood. You could hear the sticks strike and roll on the floor, then the men yelled out at one another for a minute; then it got dead still. Sometimes you hear like a man walking, and sometimes it sounds like something else. One night it sounded like a goat or a cow brute had got in the kitchen. You could hear like hoofs on the linoleum—not a human sound, you could tell."

"We had the door shut into the kitchen," Wilson's mother commented. "Mostly we kept it shut, and hoped it would stay; but it didn't."

"It just opened," Mr. Wilson nodded. "There wasn't a thing in there that you could see. The door just unlatched itself and opened on us."

"It ain't an easy thing to live with," his mother sighed.

"But not as bad as some of the rest," he pondered. "I don't reckon any of that could hurt you. Now there is a noise like somebody dropping an anvil or something heavy made of iron. It shakes the house when that falls."

"It fell on the bed one day," the mother breathed.

"Yes," he agreed. "That is what finished me with the house. I was bone tired and I laid down in my clothes to rest a little. Mother was setting there looking at a magazine, when all of a sudden, whump! Down comes that thing on the bed right beside me! You couldn't see nothing on the bed—just the deep dent in the mattress where it was laying. I got up out of there!

"It made a deep hole," his mother confirmed. "That thing must have weighed more than a person, for it dented the bed down deep and sagged the springs. I figure it was what sounds like an anvil, and I'd hate to think what it would do to a body if it was to fall on him."

The sun was shining brightly as we sat in the fine old room, but both occupants seemed tense. Their eyes showed plainly that they were terribly afraid.

"Did you ever see anything at all?" I insisted.

"Yes," the man breathed. "That was the worst of all. Thank God, it was only once. It came from in there, in the kitchen."

"We heard that awful, slow, thumping walk that ain't human. We had the door bolted that night. The sound came up on the step and stopped. We set dead still and prayed that the bolt would hold. The light was on and we saw the door crack open slow when the latch went back. It opened slow. We looked for something tall to be in the doorway, but it stepped up into the room not much taller than your knee, and stood there feeling around with its snout, smelling...."

"Snout!" I gasped.

"Or trunk, or what you might call it! It made us think of an elephant, you know, a long, naked, snakey trunk that writhes around."

"It was like a rat, too," the mother shuddered. "But it wasn't like any right animal in God's Creation! It kept feeling around with its snout, smelling us out. It had eyes but it didn't act like it could see. And it stepped up into the room. I recollect I thought if it touched me my heart would stop beating. It didn't make any move toward us, but just stumped across the floor, slow and awful, till it got to the hearth. Then it just sunk down into the floor. It was gone—never a sound except its feet on the hard floor."

I tried to secure a more complete description of the apparition, and drew sketches. What emerged was a grotesque gray thing with a swollen body and heavy legs, the front pair longer than the back ones, a ratlike head and short hairless tail. They agreed that it had had a wrinkled, scabrous hide, studded with bristly, stiff hair—like no right animal in God's Creation, as Mrs. Wilson said of it. Apparently it stood almost three feet tall, and was about as long. Hearing it described, it was easy to believe that the devils and demons of medieval art were not entirely fanciful. It gives the unknown realm of such nightmares a particular horror.

I am convinced that a man was murdered with the broad ax in this house, that his rifle was hidden under the barn and his body thrown into the old well. However, I cannot account for the persistence of any form as hideous as the thing that burst in upon the Wilsons that fearful night. The heat and fearful sound of hooves conjure up the thought of hell and its denizens, but no rational person can believe that demons haunt the habitations of men. If it is a human soul in this hideous embodiment, then the hell of theology can actually exist.

Mr. Wilson understandably did not want this story to be made public at the time he told it to me, for he hoped to sell the house although he said he could not sell it without warning the prospective buyer.

When FATE magazine asked me to investigate the possibility of publishing the story, I hardly expected to find the Wilsons living in the old house. I was half-afraid that they might not be living at all. Therefore, when I drove up and found the house vacant, I was not surprised. The house seemed much older, far gone in dilapidation. The siding was half off, leaving the gray ribs of the house exposed. However, the grounds were neat, and I found a tenant living in the little house at the rear. He had not heard or seen anything amiss, and informed me that a Mr. Graham, who operates the welding shop two doors up the street, had bought the property. The Wilsons lived in a new house on the far side of town.

I then visited Mr. Graham, a cheerful, friendly man, who laughed when asked if the story might be printed. He said that he had bought the place for $1,800, and would sell it for $2,000, which allows very little for the worth of the old house. He said he wished that he could do something to preserve it, but doubted that he could, and that it was not worthwhile to repair it enough to attract renters. He seemed the last man alive to be concerned with ghosts or supernatural phenomena.

"It doesn't matter to me if your story makes the place appear to be the most haunted house in South Carolina," he smiled. "Spooks are about the last thing that I would let worry me any. I remember that Wilson said he saw things there but I didn't pay much attention and don't remember what he told me. The ground and the little house are worth what I ask, and the moldings and woodwork in the big room are worth quite a bit. You know, some rich woman tried to buy them to put in her own house, and another person offered once to fix up the old place fit to live in if he could take the woodwork."

I asked to see the great room once more and Mr. Graham loaned me the key to the house. Two young men were sitting in a car outside the shop, and he stepped to the door with me and spoke with them.

"Did you ever hear that the old house there was haunted?" he asked.

"Wilson always claimed it was," one replied.

"Everybody I ever heard say anything says it is, and always was," the other nodded.

The tenant of the little house accompanied me inside, as Mr. Graham was too busy. As I told him some of the details the Wilsons had told me, he smiled incredulously. "All that may be so—I wouldn't deny it—but I never did take much stock in such stuff. I never saw anything myself, here or any other place. Some folks say they do and them that can't, can't say what the others can see, what they only think they see or say they see. It's a funny thing that only a few people have the power. The rest can't see anything."

I was standing in a spot that had grown deathly cold. I motioned to him.

"Come over here where I am and hold out your arm," I breathed.

He did so, puzzled. Then he stared hard at me. "You mean the cold?"

I nodded. We both looked unhappy and ill at ease.

"I was thinking it was a draft coming up through the kitchen door from outside—but it couldn't be that. It's hot outside!"

It was mid-July and very hot.

Nevertheless, the great room had a moving spot of chill that no atmospheric conditions could explain. It seemed to follow me as I moved about in the gloom. It stopped beside me when I stood still.

I went under the house to look at a peculiar stone, like a tombstone, at the foot of the chimney, thinking that money might be hidden there. I found only a horrid sensation of something invisible, repellent, and hostile, which drove me out in short order and left me shaking, but I saw nothing and heard nothing. Mr. Wilson reported that he had such sensations often as he worked to renovate the house, particularly in the kitchen, which seems to be the room in which the worst phenomena originate.

I wonder if some day we will know why some houses hold remembered evil within their walls.

The Ghost of Brinkley College

By Michael Finger

October 1992

*There was only one good way to prove Clara—
and for that matter, the ghost Lizzie—right or
wrong. Someone must dig for the treasure.*

South Fifth Street today is a dreary industrial area of
South Memphis, hemmed in by derelict warehouses and
railroad tracks. But in 1871, DeSoto Street—as it was
then called—was a prime residential district, lined with
grand homes and shaded by stately trees. On one side of
the road, guarded by a high iron gate, stood the old
Davie place, a two-story mansion with six massive Ionic
columns stretching across the front.

157

After the Civil War it was converted to the Brinkley Female College, a boarding school for some fifty pupils of varying ages. Because of its gloomy setting—standing alone on a slight hill, within a dark grove of old trees—or perhaps the tales that old man Brinkley had gone bankrupt, then insane, after founding the college, the place had a reputation for being haunted.

A reputation that was seemingly without basis—until February 21, 1871.

On that Tuesday afternoon, Clara Robertson, the thirteen-year-old daughter of a respected Memphis attorney, was practicing her piano lessons in the long hallway on the second floor of the college. As she sat alone before the piano, she noticed a little girl ascend the stairs at the end of the dark hall, then pause at the landing. Clara thought nothing of it until the figure turned toward her, when, to her horror, she said, "I saw it was not a living thing."

As reported over the following days in The *Memphis Avalanche* newspaper, Clara said the specter was "...a girl about eight years of age, with sunken, lusterless eyes and strikingly emaciated features. Its teeth protruded from a fleshless mouth, and the hair was deep black, loose, and flowing. The object was virtually a skeleton in appearance, clad in a dingy and tattered dress of faded pink, which was partly covered with a greenish and slimy mold."

At first paralyzed with fear, the young girl ran screaming into an adjoining bedroom and jumped into bed with a sick girl there.

The ghost silently followed her and moved to the bed, where it placed a decaying hand upon the pillow by Clara's head and gently tugged at the poor girl's hair.

Unable to speak, her face jammed to the pillow, Clara could do nothing but feebly wave the ghost away with her hand. After a few unbearable minutes, the apparition finally backed away from the bed and left the room, leaving the two girls cowering under the blankets.

When she finally recovered her wits, Clara rushed downstairs and breathlessly told her fellow students what she had encountered. According to the newspaper, her excited tale was met with "belief, disbelief, and ridicule." Even if the college were haunted, her friends admitted, everyone said it was by the ghost of old Mr. Brinkley, not by a little girl dressed in pink, and certainly not during the day!

Clara told reporters she began to suspect it was just a trick of her imagination after all.

The next morning, she was again practicing the piano in the upstairs music room, this time accompanied by two other students. All three were suddenly surprised by a strange sound they described later "as if someone were dashing water to the floor." Turning towards the noise, they discovered the ghostly little girl in the gloom of the hallway behind them.

Clara reported she could see the shriveled creature very clearly; the other girls admitted they could distinguish only a shadowy outline of something—but something that was moving towards them.

The three girls fled downstairs, shrieking, and bumped into one of the college instructors, Miss Jackie Boone. After calming the frightened students, she demanded that they take her back upstairs, so she could see this strange figure for herself, no doubt thinking, "A ghost indeed! What nonsense!"

Unfortunately for the skeptical instructor, the little girl was still there, this time in full view of all. Gathering her courage, Clara cautiously demanded what the ghost wanted of them.

Pointing a ghastly finger out the window at the ground below, the creature murmured, "Five feet under a stump near this house are some valuables that you should have," now pointing to Clara. With that, the image simply faded away. Miss Boone confessed that she could hear only a vague rumbling sound, but the girls told reporters they could hear the words clearly.

Since there were more witnesses to the sighting, doubts of Clara's honesty—and sanity—began to fade. After hearing of this latest incident, her father came to the school, concerned that some person there was playing a cruel joke on his daughter. The school's principal, identified in the newspapers only as a Mr. Meredith, was likewise concerned, but for his own reasons. Joke or not, a ghost haunting his college and scaring the daylights out of students could ruin him. What proper Memphis family would send their innocent daughter to be trained in such an establishment?

The next morning, the principal gathered the instructors and pupils in the hallway and sent Clara out into the yard while he questioned them. As she slowly walked among the old trees behind the school, the specter suddenly materialized in front of her, less than a few steps away. Clara opened her mouth to scream, but the creature silenced her by raising its hand and pleading, "Don't be afraid, Clara. My name is Lizzie Davie, and I will not harm you."

According to Clara, the ghostly child related that the old college property had once belonged to her father, and the Brinkley family never had any legal right to it. Buried nearby was a large glass jar containing the true deed to the land, as well as a small fortune in coins and jewelry. After relaying a final warning—that Clara must find the jar herself—the ghost vanished.

Old-timers recalled that the mansion housing the college had been built by the Davie family before the Civil War, and that one of the little Davie girls, a beautiful child with long, dark hair, had died in the house. Some who attended the child's funeral remembered that she was buried in a pink dress and pink slippers, a singular thing since it was usually the custom then to shroud dead children in white.

News of the latest visitation and the possible buried treasure quickly spread throughout Memphis. Headlines roared: "Brinkley Female College Haunted and in an Uproar of Terror and Confusion. Singular and Thrilling Revelations." The *Avalanche* called it, perhaps prematurely, "the most remarkable ghost story on record."

At the same time, however, the newspaper wisely sent an unidentified reporter to cross-examine Clara and investigate the strange matter a little more closely. In an introduction to the interview, which spread across six columns, the *Avalanche* noted: "The reporter looked closely for wildness of expression about the eyes and apparent wandering of the mind, and tried to stagger her with questions...but saw and elicited nothing to cast a shadow of a doubt upon her belief of what she stated."

The paper further warned its readers: "Those whose consciences are weak, or those whose intellects are not as strong as this girl of thirteen, are cautioned not to read the interview."

Clara repeated to the reporter all that had occurred, although she was unable to offer any explanations:

> Reporter: "Do you believe there are such things as
> spirits?"
> Clara: "Yes, sir, for I have seen one."
> Reporter: "Whose?"
> Clara: "Lizzie is a spirit."
> Reporter: "How do you know?"
> Clara: "She told me, and I have seen her."
> Reporter: "Have you seen other spirits?"
> Clara: "I have not."
> Reporter: "You never believed in spirits before?"
> Clara: "No, sir, but I am sure I do now."

During this interview, the reporter even tried to trick the girl by asking: "Were you and Lizzie fond of each other when little children?"

> Clara: "I never knew her."
> Reporter: "Why then has she haunted you?"
> Clara: "I'm sure I can't tell."

The reporter next cornered the beleaguered school principal, who took a decidedly different stance. Mr. Meredith admitted in the *Avalanche* that, up to now, there was not a better student in his school than Clara, but the whole affair was rather sad: "While he [Meredith] had no doubt that she was honest in her statement, it was his firm belief that the alleged visitation was simply a hallucination arising from an aberration of the mind."

In short, the principal rather bluntly concluded, "The girl had no doubt gone crazy."

There was obviously only one good way to prove Clara—and for that matter, the ghost Lizzie—right or wrong. Someone must dig for the treasure.

On Saturday night, March 4, Mr. Robertson and a handful of strong men carried shovels and picks to the college grounds and, by torchlight, began slowly to turn up the ground by the stump where Lizzie had pointed. Their attempts at secrecy were futile, however.

Word immediately swept through the neighborhood that "they're digging up the treasure!" and within hours the dusty road in front of the college was packed with thousands of curious citizens.

The hard work took hours, and by early morning the big stump was finally pulled free, but there was nothing under it but dirt. Still they kept digging; five feet down, the ghost had said. It had been a long, cold night, and as dawn began to break, much of the crowd's initial curiosity turned to ridicule. Then, one of the shovels crunched against something hard. "It's the treasure!" bystanders shouted. People rushed towards the hole. No...only some old bricks that formed part of a curious archway long buried in the ground. From the dwindling crowd came mutterings to "give up the quest; the girl was obviously a liar."

Meanwhile, Clara had been carefully secluded at her home, several blocks from the college. Early that morning, she was walking restlessly in her backyard, waiting for news from the diggers, when the ghost made yet another appearance. This time, Clara wasn't frightened. The creature chided Clara for not yet uncovering the treasure.

When the girl protested that others were searching for it even as they spoke, the ghost responded, "Then you must go and search for it yourself."

Clara rushed next door and told her neighbors this latest information. After a hasty consultation, they decided that, despite her father's orders to stay home, she should go to the college after all.

"The girl's here—the girl who saw the ghost!" The noisy crowd thronged around Clara for a closer look, and it took considerable shoving and tugging to pull her to the edge of the excavation. Nothing but an open pit and a small pile of bricks showed as the fruits of the all-night labor.

The newspaper reported that Clara grabbed a spade, clambered down into the pit, and began to dig feverishly. After turning out a few spadefuls of earth, she cried out, "I can see the jar!" A gasp arose from the crowd. Clara bent down to scoop up another shovelful...and fainted dead away from the excitement. And no jar in sight!

She was carried to the porch of the college, where she soon was revived, but her father feared she was too weak to dig further. In all this confusion, Clara's father decided to hold a brief seance on the porch, using the services of a medium who was present at the digging. (The *Avalanche* identified her only as a Mrs. Nourse.) Mrs. Nourse immediately contacted Lizzie, and the ghost pressed Clara to continue her search. Clara wept that she could not—could her father dig for her? Lizzie hesitated, then said that Mr. Robertson could finish the work. But then the ghost added a curious stipulation: If he uncovered anything, "Sixty days must pass before the jar could be opened."

Mr. Robertson, assisted by the other diggers, carefully began to chip away at the remainder of the bricks that lay exposed in the bottom of the pit. After an hour more of work, they managed to open a hole in the bricks. And lying within was a glass jar!

The treasure was soon pulled free and handed up out of the pit. It was a five-gallon Mason jar, covered with dirt and mold, but through the sides everyone could see several large bags and packages, and one large yellow envelope. The missing deed to the Davie property?

Clara—and the ghost, it seemed—had told the truth after all, and the *Avalanche* related the events on a page-one story the following day: "Excitement throughout the city, especially that part of it in which the college is situated, is at the highest pitch imaginable. Yesterday and the day before, the place was visited by thousands of persons of all ages, sexes, and conditions, many of whom sought out and interviewed little Clara Robertson, the object of the alleged unearthly visitations. So great has been the rush that Mr. Meredith was compelled yesterday to solicit the aid of the police in keeping back the crowds of the curious from the college grounds, and at an early hour the entrances were placed under guard."

Mr. Robertson carried the elusive prize home with him. Clara, it was reported in a newspaper interview, was relieved by the discovery, feeling that the strange affair was probably over at last:

Reporter: "How did you feel after your Pa gave you the jar?"
Clara: "I felt real glad."
Reporter: "Because you felt rich?"

Clara: "No, because I felt Lizzie and I were out of
  trouble."

In an editorial, the *Avalanche* tried to convey a sense of the entire city's fascination: "All day long, and all through the night, the ghost was talked of wherever one chanced to go, and 'ghost' with a spoon in it was the favorite beverage in every barroom. Groups discussed the marvelous occurrences at almost every corner of the streets, and various were the theories suggested and the wonderful experiences related."

The next day, Mr. Robertson announced that he would satisfy the public's curiosity in full view of all. At the end of the sixty-day waiting period requested by Lizzie, both he and Clara would open the big jar on the stage of the city's Opera House. There would be a $1 admission fee, a rather hefty sum in those days, with half the proceeds going to Clara to compensate her for her ordeal. Mr. Robertson said he planned to donate the remainder to the city's Episcopal Church Home for Orphans. (At least that was the intention. The good bishop there quickly declined the offer; he would have nothing to do, he said, with "ghost money.")

Sixty days. A dreadfully long time to wait for the solution to the mystery. As it turned out, the strange affair came to a sudden and dramatic end.

A few days after the discovery, on a dark night in March, Mr. Robertson heard voices in the backyard of his home and went to investigate. He didn't return. A servant sent after him found the poor man lying insensible in the yard, with a deep gash across his head and bruises around his throat. Luckily, he was not critically wounded, and by the time a doctor arrived he had regained his senses.

Robertson later told reporters that four "ruffians" had seized him in the yard and forced him to confess the hiding place of the jar. Of all places, he had concealed it under the seat of the outhouse, dangling by a rope. After nabbing the treasure, one of the thieves grabbed him by the neck and struck him over the head with a knife, knocking him out.

The treasure was gone, and no trace of it ever surfaced again. The missing deed, if indeed it was inside the envelope in the jar, was never used as Lizzie had intended, and the other objects in the jar would remain unknown.

There's no record, unfortunately, of what became of Clara, her father, and the others involved in this incident. Perhaps, after all the excitement died away, she returned to the college and tried to lead a normal life. No doubt Mr. Meredith was relieved that his school no longer had a pink specter haunting it. And as for Lizzie, if she did appear again, no one—certainly not Clara—ever mentioned it.

The college itself went through hard times in later years. After the school closed early in this century, the old house became a tenement for railroad workers, and the other homes along the street came down one by one as the neighborhood slowly declined.

For years the old place stood alone on the street as a faded specter itself, a gray ghost of a bygone age, until it was finally torn down in 1972.

Murderer Reappears After 200 Years

By Ervin Bonkalo

April 1988

A history-minded tourist, interpreting a night-mare, devises a scenario from slavery days which turns out to be historical fact.

In the summer of 1979 we planned a trip from our home in Canada to the United States because my wife Maria-Luise wanted to visit an aunt, Klara Fritze, who was in a home for the aged in Gettysburg, Tennessee. We booked a reservation in a motel well ahead because that city is overrun by visitors every summer.

We arrived there on July 5 and I liked what I saw of the motel's exterior. As a historian I am always interested in old buildings and I saw at first glance that the main building in the short section of the U-shaped motel was very old, eighteenth-century style. Built of solid gray stone with white-trimmed sixteen-pane windows, it was two stories high with a small domed bell tower crowning the roof above the centrally situated door.

Although it was only 5:00 P.M. we learned to our great dismay that our reserved room had not been held for us. (As a general rule in American motels and hotels, a reserved room can be rented if a guest does not occupy it by six o'clock unless he telephones to say that he will arrive late.) Chagrined, the manager telephoned all the other motels and guest houses in the city and within a twenty-mile radius but nothing was available.

"Look," said the manager, "we have one room which we usually don't rent because it is the last one in the east wing and it faces the street. It has two windows to the street and one window and its entrance door opening on the courtyard. It has no air conditioning, only a two-piece bathroom, no shower or bathtub and it is noisy. I'll rent it to you for half the usual price."

We were too old to pitch a tent at some campground and that would not be air-conditioned either. Tired from the long drive, we accepted the manager's offer and, with our toy poodle Fleur, moved in. The large square room felt rather cool when the door was opened and it had a slightly musty smell. Never mind—we would endure it for one night. Tomorrow we would visit Aunty, then move on to a small resort in the Smoky Mountains where we were to spend the rest of our vacation.

We went out for dinner and when we returned we found Fleur not in her basket but in a corner, shaking. The poodle accompanied us on all our trips in Canada and the United States. We could leave her in the motel room for hours. She never made a mess or a sound even if the motel personnel entered the room for some reason. But if anyone touched our luggage he had to flee in a hurry!

Something must have scared the poor animal. All evening as we were unpacking and preparing to go to bed, Fleur kept close to my feet, walking along with me. She had never done this before; she was afraid of something.

The room had two narrow beds with a night table between. I left the courtyard window open, hoping that it might get a little cooler during the night. My wife chose the bed nearer that window. It was then I noticed that the windows facing the street were not like the one facing the courtyard. Those had twelve panes with white-painted wood trim separating them, a window style that was made until the 1880s when the manufacture of panel glass began in America. Until then panel glass was mainly imported from England or was made by hand in glass-makers' workshops.

"Ah!" I thought. "This room is not part of the new motel. It must have been here long before. I'll have to take a good look tomorrow morning."

I took Fleur out for a short walk but could not see much of the contours of the section in which our room was situated because an old tree shaded it from the street-lights. I did notice that the roof was not flat as it was over the motel wings. It had a gable facing the street and the roof was slanted accordingly.

Returning from our walk, Fleur dug in all four feet and resisted the pull of the leash. "Why is she doing that?" I wondered. "She must be afraid of something in that room." I picked up the three-pound dog, carried her in and put her in her basket close to my bed where she curled up.

When I went to bed and switched off the bedside lamp, the full moon was shining through the windows facing the street and only the branches of the old tree provided some shadow. The street was not as noisy as the manager had predicted. Hardly any cars passed by. Soon we were all asleep.

Suddenly my wife's screams awakened me. I switched on the bedside lamp and got up to find her sitting up in bed staring with wide-open eyes toward the courtyard window and shaking.

"What happened?" I asked.

In a trembling voice, she said, "A black man—half-naked—he had a large knife between his teeth—jumped in through the window. He wanted to kill me...."

I embraced her and said, "It was a nightmare. Lie down and go back to steep."

But she insisted, "I was not sleeping. The noise of someone trying to remove the screen woke me up. I saw him, J saw him...."

Then I noticed the dog. Fleur was sitting in the far corner of the room, trembling and crying. "She must have seen it too," I thought. Then I said, "I'll leave the lamp on and sit up all night. If I hear anything suspicious I'll call the manager." Only then did I notice there was no phone in the room.

It was past 2:00 A.M. Soon Maria-Luise went back to sleep. Fleur curled up in my lap and slept too. As I kept vigil I mused about what had happened.

In early July the nights are short, the daylight long. When dawn came I dressed, put Fleur in her basket and tiptoed out.

Nobody was around and the street was deserted. By now I was certain that the wing where our room was located had been a house and I looked for evidence of this. The doors of the motel rooms faced the courtyard formed by the U shape. On the outer side, which faced a tree-studded ravine, only the small squares for the bathroom windows had been cut through the walls. But in the building containing our room I noticed two basement windows—but the motel had no basement. Between these windows stone steps led up to a clearly visible door frame which had been filled in with red brick.

I spent a long time observing the exterior of the motel and came to the conclusion two buildings on the property were original—the main house and a small house about 300 feet east of it. The background of Maria-Luise's nightmare began to take shape in my mind. A historian reads a lot, sees more than other people do, and acquires a way of thinking that we call "history-mindedness."

The manager was in his office when I called on him at 6:45. He recognized me and said, "Any complaint? I told you...."

I interrupted him, saying, "No complaint, but we had a very interesting night. Before I speak about that I want to say a few things about the original buildings of your establishment. Before the motel was built—about 200 years ago, in fact—a rich plantation owner lived in the house in the middle. The room where we slept is in a little house which was the quarters for the female slaves."

The manager interrupted me, "I know all that. Are you a member of the historical society?"

"No, I am not," I said. "I am a teacher from Canada. While I know as much about the Civil War and American history as a Canadian history teacher must know, I have never read anything about the pre-Civil War history of this area. All that I've said is my educated guess."

"That's remarkable!" he replied, shaking his head. "How much more do you know?"

"The plantation owner or his son ordered a black servant girl to sleep with him. She reluctantly agreed because she would have been severely punished or sold if she refused, never to see parents or lover again. Yes, she had a lover, one of the black male servants. One night the jealous lover went to the female slave house through the window and killed the girl with a knife. My wife saw the scene in a nightmare which she had last night."

The manager stood up and looked at me in amazement, then went to his bookcase, removed a slim paperback, and asked, "Are you sure you have never read this book?" It was *The History of the Bucknell Plantation*. "My grandfather wrote it," he continued. "He bought the place from the Bucknell family's last descendant."

"I've never seen it," I said. "Did what I guessed at really occur?"

"It did," he said. "Let's see, what was the date it happened? Here it is—July 5, 1779."

I was stunned. The murderer had reappeared after 200 years to the day!

The Ghost of Crazy Horse Hollow
by Leo Miller

June 1978

We had moved to the valley in search of peace and quiet, but instead we got a ghost horse that scared the daylights out of us and threw the countryside into an uproar.

I could hear the horse racing toward us down the narrow country road, its metal shoes clanged against the hard chert of the road and echoed from the steep hillsides like rolling thunder.

I pulled Crystal, my five-year-old daughter, to safety behind a large tree so the horse would not trample us as it passed. "The rider must be crazy to ride that fast down a narrow crooked road like this," I thought. "Someone could get killed if he doesn't slow that beast down."

The pounding hooves were almost upon us. I peered cautiously around the tree and waited for the animal to come around the bend in the road. It never came—but the thundering hooves did. They passed us and gradually faded in the distance.

Stunned, I attempted to understand what had happened. There was no mistaking the sounds we heard. Yet there was no way for a horse to have left the road and run that fast over the steep, heavily wooded hills on either side. And even if the animal had been able to do so, surely it could not have passed us without being seen.

I told Crystal to follow me as best she could while I ran down to the crossroads. Our road intersects another a short distance from the spot where we stood and the valley widens into open pastures for a mile on both sides of the crossing. If there was anything to be seen, I knew I could see it from there. I was determined to get a look at the idiot who was risking his mount's limbs and his own neck in the mad race over difficult terrain.

I could still hear the animal's hooves ringing against the gravel as I dashed into the clearing across the narrow creek that borders my property. The sound was traveling north on Snow Creek Road and couldn't have been more than a quarter-mile away but I still couldn't see a thing.

Crystal, running as fast as her short legs would carry her, tugged on my trousers and asked, "Where's the horsey, Daddy?"

"I'm trying to find out myself," I said. "It sounds like it is right over there on the other road. Can you see anything?"

"No, Daddy," she said, "but it sure sounds big and it's going awful fast!"

That 1968 experience was my introduction to the "ghost horse of Crazy Horse Hollow," as I came to think of it. At that time I had no idea it was a ghost and I wasted a lot of time and energy over the next few months trying to find some natural explanation for what I had heard. During the following three years the ghost made itself known to a great many people, some of whom actually saw it, before it faded away into the never-never land where ghost horses go after their mission on Earth has been fulfilled.

We had been living in the Maury County, Tennessee, countryside only a few months when the ghost first scared the daylights out of me. We had moved from the city because of our difficulties with neighbors who did not share our fondness for numerous weird pets. The geese bit children, the dogs dug up flower beds, the cats worried everybody, and our pet skunk terrorized unwary visitors.

Faced with giving up the animals or finding a suitable home for them, we bought a rough farm as close to the middle of nowhere as we could get. The area was hilly; in fact the slopes were so steep they were good for nothing but timberland. This was fine with me because I wasn't interested in farming. My wife Wanda wanted to get away from people and close to nature and Crystal was thrilled with the springs, creeks, and trees. The place was just what we all wanted and we moved immediately.

I have never been a morbid person but our farm began giving me the willies soon after we moved. The steep wooded hills blocked out most of the sunlight and kept our house in constant gloom. The wind rushed through the branches of the trees on the hilltop, moaning in an eerie way. And the gloominess of the steep hills, narrow gorges, and deep creek banks was further magnified by the frequent mists and fogs that settled over the valley.

We all felt uneasy. For the first few weeks no one said anything because each of us thought it was just his overworked imagination. One evening when the sensation was unusually strong we blurted simultaneously, "There's something evil about this place!" We laughed together, relieved that the feeling was mutual, and began to discuss the situation freely.

The very next day Crystal and I heard the horse. As soon as we got back to the house that afternoon, I told Wanda about the incident. She said she had heard the same sound and had watched from the window but had not been able to see anything.

It still did not occur to us that a ghost might be responsible, although I made a joking suggestion to that effect. So when we heard the horse a second time about a week later, I assumed that this time I would get to see it and maybe even meet a new neighbor riding on its back.

I was working at the creek about two city blocks from the house when I heard the horse coming down the road at a fast trot. The steady rhythm and clear ring of metal shoes striking gravel surface left no doubt in my mind that this was a fine animal, well trained and cared for, obviously an expensive riding horse rather than the usual farm nag common to the area.

The unseen animal galloped smoothly and evenly as it approached from the east.

By the time I got to the road, the horse sounded as if it were just around the bend, not more than 100 feet from me. Then the disembodied gallop passed right by but once again I never saw a thing. My eyes followed the sound as it faded out to the west but there was nothing there.

That did it, I did not believe in ghosts but this was too much. I threw my tools into my old truck and jumped in, determined to chase the sound and find out once and for all why I could hear the thing so clearly when there was nothing there. A dozen possible explanations racing through my mind, I jockeyed the pickup onto the road and roared after it. Two miles later and no horseman in sight, I turned off on some of the adjoining roads to see if by some quirk the sound had echoed in our hollow while the animal was miles away.

Half an hour later, frustrated and bewildered, I drove home to seek sympathy and have a tall glass of liquid nerve tonic. After the soothing effects of two straight shots I casually asked my wife, "Did you happen to see the fine horse that passed this afternoon?"

"No," Wanda said excitedly, "what kind was it? What did it look like? I heard it but just like last time I didn't see a thing!"

Two nights later a neighbor called to tell us one of our palomino ponies was out of the pasture. The man said it was a quarter horse, not a Shetland pony, but since we had the only palominos in that section it had to be one of ours.

Wanda and I loaded a halter, lead line, and a pail of grain into the pickup and drove down to Snow Creek Road where the horse had been seen. Although we searched the area thoroughly we could not find the animal. As soon as we got home again, I checked the barn and found all four of our horses munching contentedly on a bale of hay. None of them was lathered or agitated as it would have been if it had been running or jumping fences. Obviously the loose horse had not been one of ours.

Still, a horse loose in tobacco country is no laughing matter, no matter to whom it belongs, so I got a strong light and went back to the field by Snow Creek to look for the beast. But despite a diligent search I found nothing, not even hoofprints. That was strange because the ground was soft after a recent rain. Had the ghost—if that's what it was—been seen at last?

Of course I still wouldn't believe that it really was a ghost. I consoled myself with several logical explanations such as a trick of moonlight or a practical joke and went to bed—but not for long.

The phone rang again just as I was beginning to doze off. This time the call was from Betty Hill, who lived on our road about a quarter-mile west of us. She was mad and her angry message quickly cleared my head of its sleepy stupor. Our horse was tearing up her garden, snorting in her bedroom window and clattering around on her back porch, she announced.

I wasted no time in getting dressed and was still pulling on my trousers when I climbed into the truck. Three minutes later I was at my neighbor's house, where any sign of a horse was conspicuously absent. A careful search resulted in a complete blank. No horse, no tracks, no mud on the porch, nothing at all.

Betty, who had been waiting for me and came out as soon as I pulled into her driveway, was beside herself. She couldn't figure out what had happened to the animal. She knew it had to be somewhere. We searched again without luck and she apologized for getting me out of bed. "Must have been dreaming," she said.

"It was probably the ghost again," I suggested, now only half-jokingly. She muttered something about only nuts believing in ghosts and stomped off into the house.

While all of this was going on Wanda had checked the barn. All four horses were there. Always more open to the possibility of paranormal phenomena than I am, she concluded that I was indeed chasing a ghost. Once back inside she considerately fixed another strong dose of 90-proof nerve tonic and had it ready when I walked through the door. The look on my face explained all.

"It's time we tried a new approach to the problem," she said. By this she meant we might as well acknowledge that we were dealing with a ghost.

Things changed for the better as soon as I accepted the unacceptable. People naturally thought we were crazy for believing in ghosts but our decision certainly made the situation less aggravating. Instead of chasing a phantom I counted noses at the barn whenever a report of a loose palomino came in. I started befriending the creature instead of ducking behind a tree every time I heard it clapping down the road. It didn't worry us at all that it might be a ghost.

The next time I heard it trotting my way, I called, "Whoa, fellow!" By golly, it did just that. It stopped just like any well-trained animal. I still couldn't see it but knowing where it was supposed to be, I started to move in that direction. As I did so, I muttered reassuring words such as "There, there, fellow, don't be nervous. Everything is all right." When I was almost to the spot where the ghost should have been, I heard a horse shuffle about and go back up the road to the east at a comfortable gallop. That was the first time I had heard it reverse its direction but it wasn't the last.

Winter was upon us in earnest by this time so we didn't spend any more time outside than was absolutely necessary. Maybe the ghost was inactive during the cold months or maybe we just didn't hear it. All remained quiet until the following spring when our ghost returned. I angered several of my neighbors when I refused to chase the ghost (which they of course assumed was one of my horses) but that didn't bother us particularly. In fact, I looked forward to its visits and went out of my way to get close enough to talk to it at every opportunity.

I had concluded in my imagination that it was the ghost of a war-horse killed in the Civil War. I speculated that it was trying desperately either to find its dead rider or to complete its mission. I wanted to put its soul to rest. Yes, I know that sounds silly, maybe even stupid. Many people have told me that in no uncertain terms. But I had developed a real affection for the creature and pitied it in its hopeless quest. I felt compelled to do all I could to relieve its suffering so that its soul could rest in peace.

As a scoutmaster I often brought the troop to my place for a camp-out. We had designated a hilltop as a permanent camp so that the boys could construct structures such as tables, shelters, showers, and anything else they chose.

One evening in June 1969 we were camped on the hill and busy with various activities when we heard a car horn beeping S.O.S. No one paid any attention at first since many of the scouts were tenderfeet and couldn't read Morse code and I had the older boys in a huddle laying plans for pranks we intended to pull on the new boys after I had told them a gruesome ghost story at an old log cabin nearby. It took several minutes for the constant beeping to soak into my addled brain. Three shorts, three longs, three shorts—Morse code for S.O.S.

Suddenly I heard it and realized that someone was trying to get us off the hill. I called the boys together and we took the shortest possible route home by skidding straight down the steeply sloping hillside.

J. K. Langston, a committeeman for the Boy Scout troop who often served as my assistant scoutmaster, was still tapping out his S.O.S. as we dashed madly up the driveway. He said Wanda had been giving him directions to our campsite when the two of them heard a horse jump over the fence and run down the road toward Snow Creek. Wanda had saddled her horse and gone after the runaway but she wanted some help in case it proved difficult to capture.

The scouts headed for the creek on foot, while I went to the barn to count heads in my herd. The only one missing was Wanda's mare and she was riding it. I asked J. K. again about what he had heard. He insisted he had definitely heard a horse clearing the fence in a running jump.

I started up the old truck and headed for the creek to help with the search just in case one of the neighbors' horses had taken a shortcut across our pasture. I found Wanda and the scouts down by the creek. They had formed a big circle and closed in on the area where the horse was supposed to be, but they found absolutely nothing when the trap was sprung. All of them had heard the animal distinctly and were positive it was in the circle they had formed, but no one could see it.

I asked if anyone had heard it run off, jump the fence, or make any other sounds after they had closed in on it. No one had heard anything so I ordered the boys on the north side to open the circle and come around behind those on the south. Then I walked very slowly and carefully into the circle and started crooning my reassuring words. "It's okay, boy, nobody is going to hurt you. Everything is just fine. You can go home now. Turn around and go on back home."

The scouts gaped in astonishment as an invisible horse shuffled its feet and galloped off down the road heading east. I never got to tell the boys the ghost story I had planned for that evening. After having participated in a real ghost story, I doubt that they would have been interested anyway.

The ghostly appearances continued for another year but less frequently and less dramatically. Whenever I could, I would talk to the animal and on several occasions had the impression that it was listening to my every word. Two or three times it actually followed me as I did chores along the roadway or by the creek.

The following spring the ghost horse did not reappear. That was the last we ever heard of it. I can only speculate about what happened to the phenomenon. Maybe it just wore itself out. But I like to think that I had something to do with setting the restless spirit at ease. I hope now that it is resting in peace.

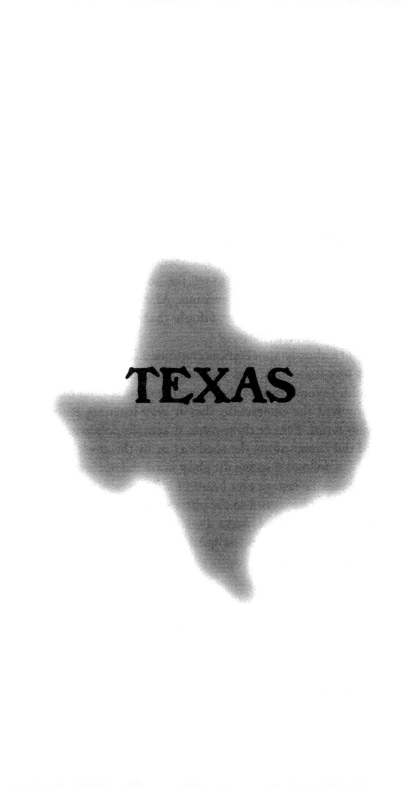

TEXAS

The Ghost of the Alamo
by Nick Howes

September 1994

Do the spirits of the brave men who defended the Alamo from Mexican attack still roam the mission fortress?

On March 6, 1836, a massed ground attack by Mexican regulars breached the walls of an old Franciscan mission that was being used as a fortress. The mission was known as the Alamo. Within minutes, the soldiers of General Antonio Lopez de Santa Anna swept through the Alamo, killing every armed defender in a bitter combat. This ended thirteen days of siege.

Among the dead were Lieutenant Colonel William Barret Travis, 26, a quick-tempered lawyer and the author of impassioned appeals to the outside world; Jim Bowie,

40, commander of the volunteers, a slave trader, entrepreneur, land speculator, and wielder of the deadly Bowie knife, and Davy Crockett, 50, world-famous frontiersman, former congressman, and a lively symbol of rough-and-ready America. Santa Anna ordered the 184 dead Texans buried in a mass grave.

In the meantime, he prepared to strike out for the north in search of General Sam Houston. Houston was raising an army, using the time the Alamo's defenders had bought.

The Alamo stood silent, secure in enemy hands. But tradition says that the defenders continued their resistance, even from the grave.

It is one of the least-known stories connected with the Alamo, and an authentic ghost story.

The legend is recounted in a 1917 book by Adina de Zavala, titled *History and Legends of the Alamo and Other Missions In and Around San Antonio*. De Zavala notes that the story is taken from a folk tale, which claims the incident occurred after Santa Anna's capture at the battle of San Jacinto, shortly after the fall of the Alamo. Mexican General Andrade ordered the mission razed. Only rubble should remain where the Texans had defied Santa Anna's army.

Demolition began without incident. But when attention was turned to the walls themselves, ghostly hands protruded from them, brandishing lit torches that sent the Mexican engineers running in terror.

Accompanying the flaming torches was a spectral verbal warning: "Depart! Touch not these walls. He who desecrates these walls shall meet a horrible fate. Multiple afflictions shall seize upon him and a horrible and agonizing and avenging torture shall be his death."

The tale claims that several relays of engineers sent to demolish the mission were frightened off by the apparitions. Whatever the truth of the story, the Alamo was not demolished.

De Zavala wrote, "The Alamo was dismantled of its works, guns, etc., the fosse filled up, and the pickets torn up and burned, but only the single outer walls of the mission-square were injured."

The man most directly responsible for the destruction of the Alamo's second story, De Zavala noted, was subsequently killed, "entombed alive and consumed by flames." Or at least, that was the common claim of those telling the tale.

Mama Buried the Haunted Bone

By Florence Emick

March 1979

She flung the closet door wide open and saw it at last—a hulking shape without face or features.

In the autumn of 1932 my parents, Eliza and Lonnie Williams, my sister Irene, and I were living in Phoenix, Arizona. Our home was near a place where the highway made a blind curve crossing over a railroad, the scene of several fatal accidents.

Early one November evening a cold drizzle set in and visibility was so poor that the headlights of the few cars on the highway were only dim haloed blobs. As we all sat around the fireplace, lulled into drowsiness by its comforting warmth, we heard the plaintive wail of the 9:00 P.M. fast freight approaching the blind curve crossing. Moments later came a thud followed by the rending, grinding sounds of metal on metal. We knew immediately it was a wreck at the crossing.

Daddy sprang to his feet and grabbed his hat and coat. "I'm going to see if I can help," he said as he dashed out and jumped into our Nash sedan. Shortly after he left, the scream of sirens came to our ears, but it was nearly a half hour before we heard the puff and chug of the freight pulling out to continue its run. Daddy came home half an hour after that.

His face was pale and he seemed exhausted as he told us about the terrible collision. The fast-moving freight had struck a car which apparently had stalled on the tracks. The car and its occupants were totally demolished. The bodies had been so mangled that at first it was hard to tell how many there were. The dismembered bodies of three or four persons were strewn along the deep brushy ditch beside the tracks. Searching for remains with his flashlight Daddy had found a severed head about a quarter mile down the tracks. He had taken off his coat and used it to carry the bloody remains up the bank. The next day Mother took his bloody coat out of the car and destroyed it.

About a month after the accident Daddy lost his job in Phoenix and decided to move back to Texas to take up farming. We didn't own any furniture so we just loaded our clothes and personal things into the Nash for the trip.

Travel by car was not as fast then as it is now. We had to spend several nights in "tourist cabins" before we reached our destination. On our first overnight stop east of Coolidge Dam, something odd happened. The Nash was parked near the front door of our cabin and sometime during the night I awoke and saw a light moving slowly around inside the car. I woke Mother who also saw it. Thinking someone was ransacking our belongings, she awakened Daddy. He too saw the moving light when he looked out the window and he then took his revolver from under his pillow and shouted, "Who's there?"

The light continued to move back and forth in the front seat. Cautiously, Daddy went out, gun in hand, but as he reached the car the light disappeared. The rest of our journey (to Rock Springs, Texas) was uneventful.

In Rock Springs our father arranged to rent a farm eight or ten miles east of Kilgore. We had been living there about six months when Daddy himself had an accident while driving home one night along the narrow road.

He told us later that as he approached a sharp curve he thought he saw a light in the back seat. Startled, he took his eyes off the road for only a moment—but it was long enough for him to miss the curve and hit the guardrail. Except for that guardrail the car would have tumbled into a deep ravine.

After the Nash was repaired Daddy decided to sell it so Mother went out to give it a thorough cleaning. When she swept under the seat she found a piece of dry bone roughly an inch long with wisps of reddish hair adhering to it. She brought it in to show to Daddy who studied it carefully, grimacing. It was a piece of skull fragment from the night of the train wreck. They didn't know what to do with it. Should they send it back to Arizona? To whom—and how? Until they could decide Mother put the piece of bone in a little tin box and placed it carefully on a shelf.

A few days later she found the piece of skull lying on the floor although the box was still on the shelf. She was very angry and thought I had meddled with it—but I had not.

"We're going to have to do something with this thing," she told Daddy. "At least take it to the garage." In the garage, some distance from the house, Daddy placed the box with its macabre content on a high ledge under the eaves.

About that time my older sister Irene and her husband separated and she came home to live. For several months the piece of skull in its little box was forgotten—until one night when Irene heard someone moving around in the house. She awakened me and we went to wake our parents. Irene told them she had heard a soft shuffle of feet on the hall floor going into the kitchen. She was afraid it was her estranged husband trying to slip up on her.

Daddy got up angry as a bear. He threw on all the lights in the house but found no one. The next day, however, the box containing the piece of skull was lying on a bench in the garage. I was with Daddy when he found it. As he put it back on the high shelf he said, "Don't tell your mother." Later I forgot and I did tell Mother.

"My goodness," she said, annoyed, "we're going to have to get rid of that thing."

She and Irene talked it over and decided the best thing to do was to bury it. With me tagging behind, the two of them went to the grassy hillside behind our old farmhouse where Mother dug a shallow hole, placed the tin box in it and covered it. That should have been the last of the troublesome bone.

A few nights later I had just gone to bed and was getting drowsy when I saw something floating in the air above me. Enough moonlight shone through my open window to light the room and all at once I realized I was looking at the piece of skull. I screamed in terror and jerked the covers over my head.

Nobody believed me—they said it was a nightmare. The next morning I kept insisting I hadn't been dreaming so Mother and Irene took me to where the tin box had been buried, all the while chiding me because I had seen them place it there the first time. To my horror and dismay, there on the ground lay the piece of skull. The ground did not look disturbed but when they dug up the box it was empty.

Daddy was very angry when we told him about this. He blamed me, saying I must have told the boys at the neighboring farm about the bone and they had dug it up as a prank. Mother argued that Daddy had not done the right thing in the first place; he should return the piece of bone to someone in authority.

"All right! All right!" Daddy finally shouted. "I'll take it to the sheriff's office and see what he thinks should be done." He put the box in his pocket and went to town.

We all breathed a sigh of relief and for a while none of us thought any more about the piece of bone. It was gone and that was all we cared about—until one night Daddy's shouting awakened us all. "Who's there? Answer me or I'll shoot!" He was standing in the hall in his nightshirt, gun in hand.

"Somebody was in here," he said. "I saw the burning end of a cigarette."

"Now, Lonnie," Mother said, "prowlers don't carry lighted cigarettes." She also pointed out that there was no odor of cigarette smoke in the room and finally succeeded in getting him to return to bed.

A few weeks after that incident Mother finished some ironing and went into the bedroom to put the clothes in the closet. As she hung them on their hangers she suddenly began to suspect someone was hiding in the closet.

Mother was not one to imagine things. She flung the closet door wide open and pushed the clothes aside so she could see all the way to the back wall. In the far corner was a dark, bulky shape—no race, no distinguishable features, just a black, hulking shadow. She screamed and ran from the room.

Daddy seemed greatly upset by her outburst and her account of what she had seen. We gathered around while he examined the closet carefully. He found nothing—but then he reached up to a top shelf and brought down a box. It was the tin box with the skull fragment in it!

Shamefacedly he admitted he'd lied about taking it to the sheriff. He said he had tried to throw the box away but found he couldn't do it. Finally he had brought it back home and hidden it in the closet.

Now Mother said firmly, "I'll show you what we'll do. And we will all do it together."

That night she put the little box on the table with our family Bible beside it. Then she lit a candle and left it to burn all night.

The next morning we all went together to the grassy hillside behind our house. We said a prayer and then Daddy dug a deep hole and gently and permanently laid the box and its contents to rest.

Spectral Nun Warns of Death

by Dorothy Bonner

November 1956

The figure of a nun had warned of death many years before. Now I saw her coming slowly down the stairs.

My Mother once told me of an incident which occurred in her childhood. It frightened her and remained vividly in her memory all her life.

When her grandmother lay dying in an upstairs bedroom Mother was sitting alone at the foot of the stairs. She was only six years old and did not understand the sad event that was taking place upstairs but, of course, the hushed comings and goings of relatives, the solemn faces, and the unfamiliar silence impressed her. It was nearly midnight. She had begun to feel forgotten when a shrouded figure came slowly down the stairs. The figure brushed past her and she realized that it was a nun. The face was averted and without a sound it disappeared through the doorway. For some reason it frightened her and she cried out in terror. Her mother came down to her, sobbing and asking her to be quiet. Her grandmother had just died!

She told her mother about the figure but was assured that no nun had been in the house. Her relatives attributed the apparition to a child's overwrought imagination. The incident was forgotten—by everyone except Mother.

And after Mother told me this story I also forgot it, until years later. When my mother was dying I had good reason to recall it.

When I realized that Mother's illness would be fatal I had her moved from the hospital where she had been getting only perfunctory care (it was soon after the end of World War II, and there was a great shortage of nurses) to a Catholic sanitarium where the nuns were reputed to be attentive and skillful nurses. Only patients with lung diseases were eligible for admittance. Because Mother had lung cancer she was taken in.

Her room and its outlook were pleasant. The nursing care was excellent. At night, however, lay nurses took over the care of all of the patients and here the shortage was evident, too. It was seldom possible to obtain a special night nurse so I received permission to remain with my mother every night.

We were in West Texas, several thousand miles from our home in New England, so mine was a lonely, unrelieved vigil. Toward the end of the fourth week, I was sitting beside mother's bed, reading. She had just been given a hypodermic injection and seemed to have settled into a painless sleep. I remembered suddenly something I had forgotten in my concern over her suffering. The next day—November 17—would be her birthday.

I asked a nurse in another room to relieve me for a moment and I ran down to the desk to talk to the woman who was on duty there until midnight. I inquired about a florist who might deliver flowers in the morning (we were several miles outside of the city) and jotted down the information given me. It was almost midnight and she was going off duty, so I bade her goodnight and went through the hall to a rear staircase which led to Mother's room.

At the foot of the stairs I looked up and saw a nun coming slowly down toward me. Her head was bowed. Her hand slid along the railing. I could not see her face but I felt that she was experiencing great sorrow or that she was ill. I stepped aside to let her pass and she continued to move at a steady but infinitely slow pace. I wondered whether I should offer assistance but before I could speak she turned toward the door which led outside. I felt suddenly uneasy. The doors were locked at night and I couldn't imagine her intention. Her hand was on the knob—and then she was gone! The door hadn't opened, yet, she had gone through it.

Now I was thoroughly frightened. I raced up the stairs, alarmed by a terrible thought. When I reached my mother's room, the nurse was watching for me, her eyes wide. "I'm afraid she's going," she said.

As I stepped into the room, Mother opened her mouth as though to speak and died.

VIRGINIA

We Live with Restless Spirits

By Barbara S. Guthrie

May 1981

*At first we heard only the sounds. Then we began
to see our ghostly tenants and sense the evil they
brought with them.*

It is a lovely house, situated in a beautiful location near
Salem, Virginia, where we have all the privacy we want
without being cut off from the rest of the world. It was
our dream come true—we had planned the house for
nearly fourteen years. But after we moved in on April 15,
1971, we discovered the house had some strange sur-
prises in store for us.

At first they were just little things. Our very first night in the house I was awakened at 3:00 A.M. by weird music with no apparent source. At first I thought I was dreaming. The music was unlike any I had ever heard. A man was singing and the sound resembled something recorded long ago.

That first night I was the only one who heard it. I didn't want to wake the others. But two nights later, when it woke me again at 3:00 A.M., my husband Jim heard it, too. As I had done the first time, we checked the radios, the television, and the stereo to make sure nothing had been left on. Nothing had.

We heard it one more time after that and to this day we have no idea where it came from.

From the beginning we felt an eerie atmosphere pervading the place. We couldn't understand it; after all, the house was brand new and we were the only people who had lived in it. But we learned the strange occurrences weren't restricted to just the house. In the years to come many of the phenomena took place outside.

The second such occurrence happened about two weeks later. Early one morning I went outside to the carport to transplant some potted plants. My nephew, Christopher Smith, who was three years old at the time, was playing in the front yard and I could see him from where I worked. I was deep in thought about what I wanted to plant in my flower bed when all of a sudden a shadow fell over my shoulder. I was squatting, facing the front yard, and I could see Christopher, so I knew it wasn't him.

When I heard the breathing I was gripped with terror. I was sure someone had slipped up behind me and I was afraid I wouldn't be able to get Christopher and run to the safety of the house. It would do no good to scream for help because no one lived close enough to hear me. I was at the intruder's mercy.

I was too frightened to move or even to look up to see who it was. Then gradually the shadow and the breathing faded away. Summoning all my courage, I looked up and around me. There was no one in sight!

I was so relieved that I nearly cried. But over the years we would experience this unnerving phenomenon a number of times.

It took a couple of weeks to get things in shape upstairs in the main part of the house before I could get started on the basement. We had a fireplace built in our basement since we planned to put a den down there later on. But for the time being we put an old sofa and chair, a few tables, and throw rugs down and fixed it up enough so that we could enjoy it in the meantime.

Around the end of the first month there we built our first fire in the fireplace. We popped corn, fixed soft drinks, and took a portable television down with us. No sooner had we settled down than it started.

At first we heard someone walking back and forth upstairs. Then doors slammed and chairs were moved. We were afraid that someone had broken into the house. Because all of our guns were upstairs where the noise was coming from, we were left defenseless.

Nonetheless Jim decided to go upstairs and check. When he returned a few minutes later and announced that no one was up there, I could hardly believe my ears.

So we settled down once more and the noise started again. Several times we went upstairs to check only to find nothing.

And that's the way it went for the next couple of years. When we were upstairs the noise was downstairs and when we were downstairs the noise was upstairs. We were not the only ones to hear these sounds; friends and relatives heard them too.

I'll never forget the day I had a new washer delivered. I had asked that it be delivered before 1:30 since at the time I was driving a school bus and had to leave on my afternoon run at 2:00. At about 1:20 the truck pulled up.

I told the delivery men to come around to the back of the house and I ran downstairs to open the door for them.

After they had unloaded the washer and set it up, they proceeded to explain how to use it. But they never got a chance to finish.

Something walked (actually stomped is more like it) back and forth across the floor upstairs. Doors slammed, footsteps sounded up and down the stairs leading from the kitchen to the basement.

One of the delivery men remarked, "Someone is sure having a time upstairs."

By this time I had grown so used to the noise that it did not frighten me. So I said jokingly, "I'll give you ten dollars each if you go upstairs and find anyone."

They looked startled. "You're kidding!" one said. "Then what's making all of that noise?"

"Your guess is as good as mine," I replied.

They were in such a hurry to leave that they forgot all about giving me directions on how to use the washer!

Up until that time only the noises had disturbed us and when we checked and found it wasn't anyone, we had shrugged the matter off, assuring ourselves that there had to be some explanation. But as the months passed and more things happened, we weren't so sure.

One day in October 1971 Jim came in from outdoors and said, "Honey, I just heard the most pitiful moan." It had come from someplace next to the carport. He heard it twice.

During the next two months our children Carmen, Crystal, and Michelle, my cousin Jimmy Rettinger, and our friend Lynn White also heard the moan. But I didn't hear it. In fact, I accused them of letting their imaginations run away with them.

Then about eight o'clock one evening in May 1972, I finally heard it. I had finished doing the dinner dishes and closed down the kitchen to go to the bedroom to read.

Jim was sprawled across the bed reading the evening paper. Crystal and Michelle, our two younger daughters, were in their bedroom doing their homework and Carmen, our oldest daughter, was preparing to take a bath. I had just slipped on my nightgown and picked up a book from my bedside table when we heard an awful noise coming from the kitchen.

It sounded as if the kitchen chairs were being scooted across the floor and the table was being rocked so hard that I thought its legs would break off.

Jim looked at me. Then he bolted for the closet to get his pistol while I grabbed my housecoat and followed him down the hallway. Just as we got to the bathroom door which opens into the hallway, we heard the most pathetic moan I have ever heard in my life.

Carmen had just stepped into the tub when the moan sounded. She grabbed a towel and nearly collided with us as we hurried into the kitchen.

I snapped on the lights as the moan sounded again. It sounded as if someone were being tortured.

The kitchen was empty—nothing disturbed, everything just as I had left it no more than fifteen minutes earlier. The only difference was that the room was as cold as ice.

Soon strange lights started to flash in different parts of the house. They were just small circles that would appear briefly and then disappear. One of these lights appeared the night my mother-in-law died.

On June 29, 1975, about 2:00 P.M. my ten-year-old daughter Michelle and eight-year-old niece Angela Clark were sitting on the kitchen floor in front of our sliding glass door which leads out to the sundeck. As they shuffled through some old records, Angela happened to look out the glass doors toward our garden which lies about 100 feet directly down from our sundeck. She saw a boy standing there and asked Michelle who he was.

Michelle, who didn't recognize him, called to Crystal, then fourteen, to come see who it was. But by the time Crystal got there, the boy had disappeared.

I arrived home about ten minutes after this happened. The girls were quite upset as they told me about the stranger in the garden.

They said they could see him clearly from the waist down but the top part had seemed transparent. Yet they could see his head and hair.

The boy was bending over as if studying the plants. Then he stood up, moved swiftly through the row, and disappeared at the edge of the garden. Never once did he look toward the house as if he was concerned about being observed. He acted as if he were somewhere all alone.

Michelle and Angela described him as being dark-skinned, having short, dark hair, and wearing blue jeans.

The only detail they disagreed about was his age. Michelle thought he was ten or twelve years old while Angela believed he was older.

The following November, at 10:30 one evening, the dogs outside began to bark. Jim went to the front door to see what they were barking at. He left the living room light off so that he could see outside more clearly.

The girls were in their beds and I was in mine when I heard him open the front door. Suddenly he exclaimed, "What in the world—?" and immediately afterwards Carmen shouted, "Daddy, something just ran past my door!"

Something ran down the hallway and I thought it was a dog. But when I called to Jim to put the dog back outside, he said, "Barbara, I didn't let the dog in."

"Then what ran down the hallway?" I asked.

By then he was standing at our bedroom door looking as pale as a ghost. "I don't know what happened," he said. "When I opened the door something brushed on my legs and ran across the room and down the hall. I had the lights out so I couldn't see what it was."

Carmen, who had joined us along with the other girls, said, "It was something black, Daddy, but it went by so fast that I couldn't make out what it was."

This time the whole house turned cold. Although we turned the heat up in every room it took several hours before it was warm again.

Twice in the summer of 1976 the young dark male was seen clearly by Carmen. Each time he vanished into thin air.

The first time Carmen saw him, she was in her room getting ready for a date. Her dresser was directly across the room from her window which looked out on our front yard. She was standing in front of the dresser mirror combing her hair with her back to the window. By looking into the mirror she could see our front yard without difficulty.

She had just put down her comb when a reflection in the mirror caught her eye.

"Mom!" she called. "Who's the boy in the yard?"

I was in the kitchen preparing dinner. "I don't know," I said. "Who does it look like?"

When she didn't respond I walked through the living room to the front door and looked out. Seeing no one outside, I went to Carmen's room. She was standing at the window looking shaken.

"Carmen!" I called.

She turned slowly to face me. "That's the strangest thing," she said. "I could see his reflection in the mirror and he was walking toward the house. But when I looked out the window he just disappeared."

Three weeks later she saw him again. As she sat on the front steps she glanced over toward our picnic area, which is at the side of our house in a small grove of pines. "He was walking through the pines one moment and the next moment he was gone," she told me.

One morning in September of that year she was on her way to school when on impulse she looked back at the house. She was startled to see a large mist forming a figure outside my bedroom window. As soon as the figure formed, it seemed to run around the corner of the house.

A few minutes later Carmen called from school to check on me. I was still in bed. I told her I had awakened to a strange tapping sound and a horrible odor in my bedroom. I looked around but never could find anything.

So when Carmen told me what she had seen I figured that explained things—sort of. That was one day I was truly afraid to be alone in the house.

The scariest thing of all happened in October 1978.

I was asleep and something—I don't know what—woke me up. For a moment I lay there listening. I could sense some kind of presence nearby. Then I heard a male voice say very clearly, "I could kill you, you bitch."

With trembling hands I switched on the bedside light. No one was there, at least that I could see, but I could feel something evil was present and I could smell a terrible stench. Finally it cleared away, but I could not sleep the rest of the night and for weeks after that I was afraid to be alone in the house.

Our children have terrible nightmares at times. We always sleep with the hall lights on because they partially illuminate each of our bedrooms.

On numerous other occasions strange things have happened in our house, far too many to record here. I don't know what causes them or what to do about them but we love our home even if we must share it with unknown, sometimes frightening forces.

Before we built on this hill, because of its seclusion it was a lover's lane. Many strange tales were circulated about it but we figured that they were mostly talk. We know better now, however.

I just pray that whatever is causing these disturbances will allow us more peace and quiet in the future than it has given us in the past.

The Ghost with the Golden Hair

By Hugh Lynn Cayce

January 1978

Why did the young woman's apparition return to haunt a tiny child she had never known? A noted psychic investigator discovered the tragic answer.

I sat up and turned on the bedside light but before I could pick up the phone it rang again. My wife Sally turned over and watched me expectantly as I listened to the voice on the other end of the wire. Both of us could see the clock on the table, which showed 12:15.

"Hugh Lynn, we need your help. We can't stand much more of this," said a man's voice which I gradually recognized as that of a friend whose wife had just come home from the hospital bringing their new baby boy with her.

"Shirley is seeing a ghost. It's happened three times already. She becomes hysterical and now she has fainted," my friend continued. "I hate to bother you at this hour but there's no one else who wouldn't think we are crazy. Could you possibly come and see her? You know we are just up the street from you."

Jack Long was a young architect, as sane and sensible as they come. He and his wife were ARE (Association for Research and Enlightenment) members. We had been in their home on one occasion for dinner. His wife Shirley was a gregarious person, mother of a lovely six-year-old daughter besides the new baby. I agreed quickly to come the couple of blocks to see them. I explained briefly to my wife that the Longs were in some kind of trouble and that I'd be right back.

When I reached the Longs' second-story apartment Jack met me at the door. Taking me into the kitchen, he pressed a cup of coffee on me and poured out this almost incoherent story.

"Shirley's mother is with her now. She came this afternoon when I called her and she helped with supper. She was here when Martha—the six-year-old—got home from school," Jack's words tumbled on as he continued.

"This afternoon Shirley called me at the office. She was hysterical. She told me she had seen a ghost. She said that she had taken a nap with the baby's crib by the bedside. When she awakened she said that the face of a blond woman with hair coiled on top of her head was just a few inches from her face. Shirley said she was so frightened that she screamed and raised up in bed. The air was ice-cold over the baby's crib."

Jack went on, jumping from one concern to another, "I was afraid our daughter Martha would be upset when she came home, so I said I'd call Shirley's mother and get her over there right away. I promised I'd be home early.

"Her mother agreed to go. She reassured me," Jack went on. "'Shirley's just had a bad dream,' she said. 'Some people are emotionally disturbed after a birth.' She told me she'd be there when Martha got home."

"I felt better," Jack continued, "until a couple of hours later when Shirley's mother called and urged me to come home immediately. She said that Shirley had been all right until she went to the bedroom from the kitchen where they had been drinking coffee and talking. She heard Shirley scream and found her sobbing with the baby in her arms. Shirley claimed that she had come to the door of the bedroom to see the blond woman leaning over the crib."

At this point I tried to calm Jack but he rushed on with his story. "I didn't really get upset enough to call you," he said, "until I found Shirley had left our bed after we retired. I found her here in the kitchen. She said she couldn't sleep. I sat down with her and we started to talk. Suddenly she looked up, screamed, and fainted. When she came to she claimed she had seen the woman with the coiled yellow hair in the kitchen doorway."

About this time Shirley and her mother and the little girl came in. I got Shirley's mother to take Martha back to her room and then began to question Shirley. She was hysterical but coherent. She had seen the blond woman three times! She couldn't stay in that apartment another night!

Gradually I began to calm Shirley down. I reminded her that ghosts are by no means always evil, nor can they hurt anyone, except through that person's own fears. I asked her about the woman she claimed to have seen. No, she said she never had known such a person and she hadn't heard any stories about ghosts in that apartment. She said she wasn't even sure she had believed in ghosts until now.

Finally, I got Shirley, Jack, and Shirley's mother to join me in a prayer for the blond lady with the coiled hair. I promised to get an ARE group to pray with them and to come back the next day.

It wasn't until I returned home about 1:30 that the story took on new significance. My wife sat up and turned on the light when I came in. "What in the world was wrong with the Longs?" she asked.

I told her the story quickly.

"Hugh Lynn," my wife said, "the Longs are in the upstairs apartment on the corner, aren't they? Do you know who lived there toward the end of the war? It was Captain Shark and his wife Cathy. She was English and was very unhappy. They had a little boy just about Tommy's age. She and I walked on the beach together. I heard after they left here that she committed suicide on the way back to England. Hugh Lynn, she had long blond hair which she wore coiled on the top of her head."

The next day I talked with Jack and Shirley again. I had asked a study group to pray for the blond lady. That was in September 1954 and she never disturbed Shirley again.

Was Shirley especially sensitive after the birth of her little boy, so that she picked up the thought form of the unhappy blond English girl? Or was the ghost trapped in the apartment looking for the little boy she had deserted in her overwrought state?

It certainly would seem Shirley saw something. And seemingly our prayers helped.

The Ghost with a Rose in Her Hair

by Eddie Harrell

January 1960

The tall woman in white was frighteningly insub-stantial—but she left a material token of her visits.

In September of 1908 my father and mother, Charles and Laura Harrell, moved into a large three-story stucco house across from the City Park in Norfolk, Virginia. The house was similar to a thousand others built in the late 1800s, planned with a large hall opening on a large parlor and dining room kitchen and pantry with a west wing built off into an L shape on the first floor, two large bedrooms and halls on each upper floor.

As I was away at school most of the time, the top floor hall room was assigned to my use when home and the large front room was reserved as a sort of den and library. The large room in the rear was occupied by two servants. Both had been with my family for more than ten years.

My parents were hardly settled in the house when both servants complained about their room and wanted to change. At first they would give no reasons, but when questioned separately they told of queer noises both at night and during the day, of mysteriously moving furniture, of whispered conversations which were perfectly audible, but could not be understood in words. Neither of the servants would enter the house alone at night, and both declared that they felt the presence of a third person in their room all the time. So at their request they were given the little hall room next to the rear chamber. In this room they were apparently undisturbed.

All this occurred while I was away at school. When I came home for Christmas I had heard nothing about it. It was not until after the incident I am about to relate that my father told me of the servants' complaints.

I had been home more than a week and slept nightly in my little hall bedroom, undisturbed from the hour of my retirement to the clang of the rising bell in the morning. However, New Year's Eve I was awakened from a sound sleep to discover that the ceiling light was burning brightly in my room. Sitting up in bed to try to ascertain why it was on (I had turned it off when I retired), I was amazed to discover a woman standing in the window alcove, looking out into the street or into the park. She was tall, slender, and dressed entirely in white, which contrasted strongly with the mass of black hair dressed high on her head. There was a single red rose tucked into her hair. She held her hand to her temple, as if to shield her eyes from the light, that she might see out into the darkness better. I could see none of her features. I spoke, meaning to inquire who she was and what she wanted, and I suddenly found myself sitting up in bed in complete darkness. The light and the lady had disappeared in an instant.

I jumped from my bed, turned on the lights, and looked about me. Everything in the room was perfectly normal and there was no evidence of anyone having entered or left it. I tried to persuade myself that I had been dreaming and reluctantly returned to bed, leaving the shaded bedside lamp on.

Next morning at breakfast I related my experience to my parents and was accused of eating too much mince pie during the holidays. However, my father cautioned me not to mention the incident to either servant or to anyone likely to tell it to them. I never did.

On my return to school I soon forgot the incident.

The following spring I returned home for the Easter holidays and occupied the same room without a thought of my mysterious visitor in white. This vacation I was in my room nearly every night, for I was behind in my studies at school and examinations were coming.

On Easter morning I was in the parlor with friends awaiting sunrise for an Easter Service (my father was a very religious man). We were having coffee and doughnuts, holding our cups high, drinking a toast to the sunrise, when one of our guests, Miss Ocie Johnson of Portsmouth, Virginia, asked suddenly, "Who was that? Someone just passed the hall door and went upstairs!"

"It must have been one of the servants," I said.

"No," she strongly persisted, "it was a young woman dressed entirely in white, with lace capelet sleeves and a long train."

I felt my knees weaken but fortunately the conversation changed and the guests were soon departing for Easter sunrise services. Just as they left, Miss Johnson turned to me laughingly and said, "You didn't tell me who the pretty brunette is you are secreting from your friends, Ed!"

"Is she really pretty?" I asked.

"As though you didn't know?" she replied.

Friends coming and going through the day gave me little time to think of the strange visitor Miss Johnson had seen. Finally evening came and I climbed the stairs to my room, where without closing the door I sat down and lit my pipe. I now remembered that it was during the New Year holiday a few months ago that the lady in white had appeared to me. At any rate I decided not to go to bed. I don't know whether I had dozed or not but I suddenly saw the figure as before at the window. I saw the long train of her dress and the lace capelet sleeves that Miss Johnson had described. The single red rose in her black hair nodded as if by a sudden movement. The lady seemed absolutely opaque and solid. No part of the window sash showed through her.

I could feel the perspiration coming out on my forehead, and although I clutched the arms of my chair tightly and was almost paralyzed with fright, I had too much pride to call out.

I finally managed to ask in an ordinary tone, "Who are you and why are you here?"

I received no reply. The figure began to disappear, not suddenly as before but slowly so that gradually I could see the window sash through her white dress. Her black hair with the red rose in it seemed to dissolve in the light of the room. Frightened as I was, the performance reminded me of the Cheshire cat in *Alice in Wonderland*.

After the lady had disappeared entirely I distinctly heard, close to my ear, a loud whisper, "Wait!" But I didn't wait. I leaped from my chair and bounded downstairs.

Eventually I returned to my room and I was troubled no further that night. Nor, in fact, did the incident repeat itself during my stay.

The following summer vacation was spent with my parents at our camp in Maine a few miles from Bangor. This was my last year in school.

During my next Christmas holiday at home in Norfolk there were several out-of-town guests at our house. All of our spare rooms were occupied and the room so shunned by our servants all these years was given to a girl cousin, Essie Mae Martin, from Washington, D.C. This Christmas was a gay one with dances and parties. On New Year's we had a dinner dance at our house. My cousin's room on that occasion was used as a coat room for the gentlemen and during the evening several of them retired there from time to time to smoke.

After the last guest departed my father and I lingered in the dining room to discuss the success of our entertainment. Essie Mae had gone upstairs to bed. When I finally started to go up, my mother informed me that she had directed my cousin to sleep in my room that night as the back room was rife with cigar smoke. I spoke of the possibilities of the semi-annual appearance of the woman in white to my father. He looked very disturbed but decided my cousin was probably asleep and it would be rude to wake her.

Father, Mother, and I finally went to our rooms. The large bedroom fell to me by virtue of the change with my cousin. I still knew nothing of the servants' objections to this room and felt only misgivings as to what my cousin might see. So I finally entered my room which was large and square. It had two windows facing north onto the back yard. The bed extended from the wall out into the center of the room toward the fireplace where a coal fire was burning in the grate. To the left of the fireplace was a marble-top table with a few books on it and between the windows was a bureau. Each side of this bureau was a bracket light and eight lights in a center chandelier hung from the ceiling.

When I finally settled on my pillow I was so tired I fell asleep almost instantly.

During the night I awoke. Every bulb in the chandelier was glowing brightly. The two wall brackets were on. In the far window stood the mysterious figure in white, now partly screened by a lace curtain. Her profile was toward me, but I could see none of her features owing to the screening position of her hands. Strange to say I was much less upset than either time before but, nevertheless, I got out of bed. As I did so I found myself suddenly in darkness, save for the feeble glow of the dying fire in the grate. I turned on the lights and seated myself in a big armchair in front of the grate wondering how my cousin fared in the next room. Presently I felt an almost irresistible desire to look behind me.

I reached for a book to distract my mind but when I opened it I was confronted by Poe's *The Raven* and with a shudder I threw it back on the table. Then I lit a cigar. After a while I fell asleep. I woke in the morning not very refreshed, still sitting in my chair.

At the breakfast table Essie Mae had hardly greeted us before she said, "I had the most remarkable dream last night, or more strictly speaking, vision, for I am sure I was awake. I awoke in the night to find the light on and I know I had turned it out. Then to my surprise I discovered that the partitions between me and the rear chamber were perfectly transparent and I could see in there plainly. Eddie was sitting in his night shirt in the big armchair before the fire. He was reading a book, while behind him stood a tall woman in white, with a red rose in her hair, and she was looking over his shoulder."

When this recital was finished my heart was racing so hard I thought it could surely be heard across the room.

Then Essie Mae added, "The red rose fell from her hair onto the floor beside Eddie's chair."

My father passed this off as a dream but after breakfast he called me aside and we went up to the room I had occupied the night before. There was a red rose as fresh as if it had just been cut, on the floor beside my chair.

It was then Father discussed the matter seriously. He told me of the aversion the servants had for the room. We decided the next time I came home we would put a watch party in each room and thoroughly investigate. But we never did. Father died suddenly of a heart attack before the Easter holiday. Mother and I moved to Washington, D.C., where we lived until December 1932, when Mother passed away.

I still have the red rose in a glass bowl. The petals, after fifty years, hold a strange freshness, seemingly a kind of petrified waxiness. The stem and leaves are dry and withered. I never touch it for fear it would crumble to dust. I do remove the glass cover occasionally.

I was in Norfolk last summer. The old house has been remodeled. I wonder if the lady in white still visits there in the wee hours of night.

WEST
VIRGINIA

Ghosts Who Named a Town

By Philip Bartholomew

October 1953

Did ghosts really name this West Virginia town?

Very few towns in the United States or anywhere else have been named after ghosts. But the tiny village of Wizard's Clip, West Virginia, commemorates poltergeist phenomena, or works of the Devil, depending on which theory one favors.

Wizard's Clip was originally known as Smithfield and is between Charlestown and Harper's Ferry on what is now West Virginia Route 51. When this highway was a winding mountain road along the west side of the Blue Ridge, in the last half of the eighteenth century, one Adam Livingstone wrestled a farm from the rugged and primeval wilderness. The site of this farm is now marked by the tiny Chapel of the Poor Souls. In 1790, after the close of the American Revolution, Adam Livingstone moved to West Virginia from York County, Pennsylvania, and a very primitive and uninhibited poltergeist moved in with him.

The trouble began when Livingstone's horses, pigs, and cows began to die from an unknown cause. They were not ill, nevertheless, they dropped dead. After Livingstone's livestock were annihilated the malevolent entity concentrated on the poultry. The chickens and turkeys followed the pigs and cows into death.

One Christmas all hell seemed to cut loose. Gifts wrapped and hidden for the coming holiday disappeared. The household cutlery was found scattered in the bedrooms. The bedding was whisked away and later found, rain-soaked, in the fields. Livingstone could not keep his fences standing. Again and again they were raised only to be broken down again. Then the attacks shifted to the house windows. The precious panes of glass were shattered and oiled paper windows were likewise destroyed. The windows had to be boarded up. If ever a man was tormented beyond endurance it was Adam Livingstone and the tormentor remained unperceived and intangible.

Local folklore states that Livingstone hated and feared the Catholics. Why this was so is not explained. However, it is said that soon after coming to Smithfield he refused to call a priest at the request of a sick stranger who died on his premises, saying, "No priest shall enter my house!" Local tradition attributes the poltergeist phenomena to this uncharitable refusal.

It is too late to examine the main witnesses and what is known of the case must be gathered from the small amount of written testimony that is left and from the stories that have been told and retold in the locality.

The phenomena lasted an unusual length of time. After Livingstone's turkeys, ducks, and chickens had gone the way of his other animals, other manifestations began. There were common poltergeist phenomena of flying stones. There were stones that rose, hung in the air, and whirled. Dishes flew and drifted hither and thither about the house, usually smashing themselves on the floor or against the walls. Adam Livingstone's devil was as versatile and malicious as the famous "Bell Witch" of Tennessee, who performed in another mountain village a generation or two later.

After the mysterious visitor apparently had tired of the stone throwing and had broken most of the Livingstone dishes it started setting fires. Fortunately these were always found just after they had started to burn and could be put out but the incendiary activity continued for some time.

Then the clipping began—the uncanny clipping from which the town got its present name, Cliptown or Wizard's Clip. (It is called Middleway on some maps.) A clipping or snipping noise, as of a pair of shears in action, was heard in the cabin. The source of the odd sound could not be found but the clicking could be heard during the day and into the night as well. Very soon the work of the "clipper" became manifest. Bedding and clothing were discovered cut, with large crescent-shaped pieces missing. Some new bolts of cloth which belonged to Mrs. Livingstone were cut to shreds. Everything in the house capable of being cut with shears was slowly sacrificed to the activity of the versatile and energetic poltergeist and its pair of ghostly shears.

These malevolent destructions continued at a variable pace for seven years in which time the Livingstone family became destitute and Adam grew increasingly desperate. At long last, after he had exhausted every means to rid the farm of its ghostly visitor, including witch doctors and country parsons, he finally went to Shepherdstown and told his trouble to an Italian named Minghini, who formerly had been a valet to General Charles Lee. Minghini sent Livingstone to see Mr. Richard McSherry who, in turn, took him to see a priest, Father Dennis Cahill. Livingstone, a Lutheran, was impressed because the priest resembled a figure in one of his dreams.

After Sunday Mass Father Cahill went with Livingstone back to his farm. It was a long trip over a very rough road. On reaching the cabin the priest told Adam that he was not permitted to exorcise the ghost or evil spirit—he had no authority to do so. However, he asked Livingstone's permission to bless the house. This was granted and Father Cahill sprinkled the doorsill with holy water and entered, reciting the prayers for the dead. That night he blessed each room, sprinkling holy water and again praying for the souls of the dead. After this the phenomena abated, but did not cease. Father Cahill visited the farm again a short time later and Mass was celebrated in the house. Now the evil phenomena ceased.

It is said the Mass was celebrated on August 21, 1797. It is said also that the entity took away the family shears when it departed but returned a sum of money which had disappeared sometime before. The shears were never found.

Soon after this Adam joined the Catholic Church and later his family followed him in his new faith.

The evil phenomena had ceased, but were replaced by a mysterious voice which admonished the family and instructed them in religion. This mysterious voice was heard by Father Demetrius A. Gallitzin, who was known as the "Apostle of the Alleghenies." He wrote an account of it in a long manuscript, now lost, and also in letters which are still in existence.

Adam Livingstone was very grateful to Father Cahill for delivering him from his evil guest and on February 21, 1802, out of his gratitude he gave thirty-five acres of his land to the Catholic Church. The deed is a matter of public record in Charleston, West Virginia, in Liber Number 1, page 152, acknowledged on June 8, 1802. It is signed by Adam Livingstone, Dennis Cahill, Richard McSherry, Joseph Minghini, and Clement Pierce.

In 1923 a chapel was built on this land and was named "The Chapel of the Poor Souls." Within its tiny nave, within its unfinished walls of native pine, Mass is said annually for the repose of the souls of the dead and has been said each year for the past thirty years. On August 21, 1952, Mass was said in the tiny chapel by an Irish priest from Hagerstown, Maryland. Likewise, Father John C. Ryan from St. Peter's Rectory at nearby Harper's Ferry observed the commemorative Mass but did not take part in it. A prayer imploring the protection of the Archangel Michael against evil spirits was included in the Mass. Thirty-nine persons from the area attended this special service. Following the Mass there was a picnic in a nearby grove. This celebration was noted in the *Catholic Digest* for September.

The story of the phenomena at Wizard's Clip is told in several old volumes which are collectors' items. It is told also at some length in a booklet of thirty-two pages titled

The Mystery of Wizard's Clip by Raphael Brown. It was first published in 1949 and is a scholarly work containing a bibliography of earlier accounts of the story from old manuscripts and books now long out of print.

It is interesting to note in this case that no exorcism was attempted. The priest prayed for the rest of the souls of the dead and whatever caused the disturbances departed. This seems to confirm the unauthenticated story of the traveler who died in the house deprived of extreme unction because of the prejudice of Adam Livingstone.

Did the stranger's resentment last for seven years, until the prayers of the dead were said for him? Or was the haunting something that followed the Livingstones from their earlier residence in Pennsylvania? The McSherry family stories concerning this case would indicate that poltergeist trouble in Pennsylvania precipitated the Livingstones' move to West Virginia.

I Guess I Saw a Ghost
By Elaine Rowley

November 1970

"...and right today a lot of people who live around here fear to travel the ridge after dark and don't even know why."

For a long time, in fact for as long as he lived, my father Ben Raines would not allow us to talk about the time when we lived on the Yost place. He had his reasons. He said it would give the place a bad name. He said nobody would believe the strange things that happened and to talk about them would reflect on our intelligence. He said the quicker it was forgotten the better for all of us. But it's been forty-four years and I haven't forgotten it yet.

Even now, when I recall our sojourn there it brings goose bumps over my arms and up the nape of my neck.

When I say I was scared almost to death that year I'm not exaggerating.

Ben Raines was a tenant farmer and a good one. He was interested in education and saved like a miser to see that his children had all the schooling possible. He had little formal education himself but he was intelligent and well-read, a fundamentalist Protestant and firm boss of his house and his children.

Thus, when my older sister Louise received her teaching certificate in 1926 and took a job in a school near Ripley, West Virginia, Father looked around for a place to live near her schoolhouse. He was reluctant to let any of us leave home. My sister Dorrie and I didn't like the idea of having Louise for a teacher but little brother Blair didn't care because it was his first year. We packed up and moved to the Yost place September 3, a few days before the school term began.

Father talked about how fortunate he was to have found a place so close to the school. The farm lay just off the Ravenswood Pike and some four miles from the little community of Sidneyville. The landlord, Jim Morgan, had bought the farm by paying up the back taxes the year before.

It wasn't much in my estimation. It looked unkempt but the fences had been repaired and the pastures cleared of stumps. The house had been vacant for a long time and it took a lot of work to get it fixed up.

I was only eleven and Dorrie was nine, but we did our share. Everybody in our household worked, played, and shared alike. We were loved and secure in the knowledge that our parents loved each other. We accepted work as part of the family plan.

The large front room of the house had been built of hewn logs. It was rather dark because its two windows looked out on a low-roofed porch which was covered at one end with wisteria vines. It had a huge well-built fireplace. Stairs came down from the single loft room which was warm and cozy in the winter from the heat of the stone chimney. Mother put Blair's bed in the little alcove formed by the chimney and Dorrie and I had the opposite side for our own. Louise had a large bedroom left of the front room and Father and Mother slept in a room on the opposite side. Mother chose that one to be close to the stairway if one of us should need her in the night.

The kitchen and dining room, having been added later, were light and cheerful.

Father surveyed the finished arrangements with satisfaction and proclaimed we would be comfortable and happy here. That was the overstatement of the year.

The first time any of us was aware something out of the ordinary was going on came one night when Mother woke me by shining a light in my face. She asked if any of us had been up. No one had.

"I could have sworn I heard bare feet slipping down the stairs," she said.

"Probably it was a rat," my father said. "Come on back to bed and I'll search him out tomorrow."

"It wasn't a rat. I sure hope we don't have a sleepwalker in the outfit," Mother insisted.

In the following weeks Mother was up often, looking for one of us parading around in the night, but Father slept soundly. Snoring gently five minutes after his head hit the pillow, he heard nothing. Neither did we, but several times I was awakened when Louise slipped into bed with Dorrie and me. She always had slept alone before. Three in a bed is a crowd and I offered to sleep with her in her own room. She'd say, "This is just fine." So I'd lie with my back against the wall and try to keep Dorrie's feet out of my stomach.

One morning Father got up at 3:00 A.M. and started to dress.

"Why are you getting up so early?" Mother asked. He was startled to see her still in bed.

"I thought I saw you go into the kitchen a while ago," he said sheepishly. "I guess it was a dream."

He went to the sink for a drink of water. When he came back he said soberly, "A streak of cold air seemed to pass me out there. Strange. There's no draft. Something about this place gives me the creeps sometimes. You feel that way?"

"Maybe the house is haunted," Mother replied.

"Tommyrot! There's no such thing as spooks. When you're dead you're dead until judgment. You don't come back. I've always had an open mind about such things and I've listened to lots of stories but I never saw or heard anything that didn't have a logical explanation if you sought it out and didn't let your imagination run wild."

"How about Saul calling on the Witch of Endor to bring back the spirit of Samuel? How about the familiar spirits the Bible tells about?"

"Humph! Go to sleep, Mary, we can have two hours' rest yet this night."

"Ben, I don't like this place." Mother was going to lay the situation on the line. "It's...well, it's unfriendly. I don't sleep good here. I feel that something, maybe the house itself, resents us. I don't want you to renew the contract with Morgan next year. I just am not going to stay any-place I feel so uncomfortable and so unwelcome."

"We'll stay if Louise gets the school again, I ain't going to have her board with other people. If there's any-thing unfriendly around here it can just shove off as long as I'm paying the rent."

Louise solved that part of the problem. She married Floyd Combs November 1, against Father's wishes, and moved in with Floyd's family until the end of the term.

The day after she left, I decided I should have a room of my own and I would take hers. After we got home from school I went in to look it over and decide where I should put my things. I stopped at the dresser to look in the mirror when a shadowy motion behind me caught my eye. I turned around cautiously. I could see nothing but I felt something was in the room with me. The only sound was the beating of my own heart. A cold chill went over me as I backed out of the room and quickly sought the company of the first person I could find. But I didn't say anything about my scare. What could I have said?

I slept in my accustomed place with Dorrie that night, understanding now why Louise used to join us. Nobody mentioned the empty bedroom and I began to shun both it and the living room. I made a bargain with Dorrie: when we had to clean these rooms we would work together. Nei-ther Dorrie nor Blair felt any different about this place than about anywhere else we had lived. We just didn't discuss things like that. Mother and Father did, maybe, but not us. Sometimes I felt eyes looking at me from nowhere—not exactly hostile eyes maybe but so alien that it was frighten-ing. The only time I liked the big front room was when we were all there on an evening with a big fire roaring up the chimney to drive out the gloom.

One unseasonably warm evening in late November Floyd and Louise were coming for a weekend visit and I was sitting at the window watching for them. I knew the way they would come. It was too muddy for Floyd's old car so they would walk up the long hollow, climb the line fence where it was nailed to the giant gum tree and cross the 300 yards of meadowland to the house.

It was just dark. I was watching for their flashlight and suddenly I saw it—a light just about the height a man would hold it as he crossed the fence. But it didn't seem right. It was too small for a flashlight and lacked the beam. It was too big for the glow of a cigarette. While I watched the light arched upward and came hurtling toward the house so fast it left a faint streak behind it. It seemed to disappear right into the walls. I turned to call Mother's attention to it but I wasn't frightened, for I didn't associate the light with anything that had happened before. Mother was talking so I turned to look at the place again and this time Floyd's flashlight was in sight.

That night after we had gone to bed Louise's screams and Floyd's exclamatory tone awakened us all. They were using her old room during their stay. Mother lit the lamp and went to investigate. All of us followed her.

Floyd's foot was wedged in the old iron bedstead. Dad had to get a crowbar to free him. Then we tried to calm Louise, who was crying hysterically.

"She jumped over me," Floyd said, embarrassed. "It woke me up so quick I thought someone was attacking us. When I jumped up I caught my foot. I don't know what scared her. I guess she had a nightmare."

"It wasn't a nightmare and it wasn't a dream," Louise sobbed. "I was wide-awake listening to a cricket and looking at the window. I saw this thin wisp of some-thing like a mist or a light smoke creeping in under the sill. I thought the house could be on fire so I watched it boil in for a minute. It suddenly poured in and right by the bed it went to whirling and boiling around until a fig-ure started to form...." She started crying again. "This place is haunted! I know it and this room especially. Things have scared me out of here before and I'm not going to sleep here tonight!"

"I don't care for haunts myself," Floyd said. "I never saw a ghost—but I ain't sleeping here either."

So they lugged their mattress to the loft and slept on the floor. I noticed Mother kept a light burning in the other bedroom that night and Father didn't object.

"Everybody's not having dreams and nightmares," Mother told my father the next morning. "There's some-thing very wrong here. It's getting us down and when you're not resting well you can get sick. If you don't find another place I will."

"I signed a lease for a year."

"Well, you go see Mr. Morgan and get out of it. Tell him the children and I won't stay here."

"I don't know anyplace to go. Besides I never reneged on a contract in my life."

"Well," Mother retorted, "I'll see what I can do about breaking the lease and you get another place or I'll burn this infernal house down!"

That very day Mother went to see the landlord. He was a genial old fellow and when Mother told him how she felt he agreed that we shouldn't have to stay if we were that uncomfortable. But he asked her not to mention around the neighborhood our reason for leaving. Mother gave him four months' rent ($20.00) and since no crops had been started no one was hurt by the deal. Mr. Morgan gave her a receipt and the contract and Mother marched home to confront my father. For the first time in their married life she had gone against his will.

She need not have been anxious about the matter. Father never said a word. He seemed relieved and set about looking for another place. But he didn't find it for a while. December was blue cold and while there was little precipitation, the ground was frozen and a north wind howled around the house without letup. Nevertheless, we experienced no more frightening incidents and enjoyed Christmas without interference.

One cold evening Father brought in some chestnuts to roast and called to Blair, "Son, step out on the porch and bring in those pine knots by the door. I'll need them in the morning to start the fires."

Blair paused in the doorway.

"Dorrie!" he yelled. "What are you doing out there without a coat?"

"I'm not out there, silly," Dorrie said, behind him.

Blair slammed the door. His face was white.

"What is it, son?" Father asked.

"I saw a girl out there looking at me. She looked like Dorrie. She had on a light dress and no shoes. She sort of went behind the wisteria vines."

Father opened the door and looked out. He saw nothing. He picked up the pine knots and came back in. "It must have been your imagination, son," he said.

The rest of the evening Blair was very thoughtful and he sat close to Mother. The old familiar chill came over me. When I went to bed I snuggled against Dorrie's plump little back and kept the covers over my head till I thought

I would smother. I would never look into the darkness again. I kept my eyes closed, afraid of what I might see. In the days that followed I grew pale and lost weight. I was beginning to be afraid even to breathe deeply. Every night I prayed that Father might soon find a new home for us and every day it seemed more unlikely.

In January the weather turned warmer—and Father heard of a vacant place about fifteen miles away. One morning he saddled a horse and because a drizzle of rain was falling he took along his slicker and rode over to check it out.

By noon the rain became a steady downpour. We began to think Father might have to stay over. To stay the night without him was more than I could even bear to think about. It wasn't so bad when he was home.

At 4:00 P.M. it was almost dark when somebody knocked at the door. I almost cried out. Mother answered the knock and there stood a very old man, miserably wet and shaking from the cold. With the warm hospitality of farm people she quickly asked him in.

"My name's Rice, ma'am, Tom Rice," he volunteered. "I was trying to reach my son-in-law's house over on the ridge. Johnny Pickett's his name. Do you know him?"

"Yes, we know him, but it's a long way to go in this rain and you're very wet. Have you had supper?"

"No, ma'am, and I do appreciate the fire. I'm pretty well soaked through."

"You could get pneumonia," Mother said. "I'll see if I can find you some dry things and I'll set you a bite to eat. We've just had supper and it's not cold yet."

"That's very kind of you, ma'am."

When he was dry, fed, and comfortable the rain still was coming down hard. Mother invited him to stay the night. We were glad when he accepted. Just to have a man around the house made us feel better—even a very old and very weak man.

Mr. Rice became quite talkative. I can still see him sitting by the fire, gently rocking in the old rocking chair with his beady black eyes fixed on the glowing coals. Wrapped in my father's work clothes he looked like an ancient Gypsy. His hands on the chair arm were like carved leather claws. How he had walked so far in the rain was a mystery to me.

"I remember this place," he said. His voice was thin and high but remarkably clear. "I lived out on the ridge beyond here when my kids were small. My wife died there. I used to come out here and help John Yost with his chores. He wasn't a man many could get along with. He fell out with the whole community before it was over. He had a different belief about things than most of us did—I just didn't bother to discuss things with him— just did my work and that was all. He kept his family to himself. Never went anywhere and never let his wife and daughter go anywhere either."

He watched the fire in silence for a while as if he had drifted back into the past, reliving his memories. Then suddenly he took up the story exactly where he left off.

"I never could forget Nora. That was his daughter. She was nigh onto thirteen, I guess, and as pretty a girl as ever lived. Pity, so few ever saw her. She was a frail girl and as I said she was about thirteen when she sickened and died. Mrs. Yost almost died, too, but it was only from grief over the way John was. He wouldn't bury Nora in the graveyard. Me and him made a coffin and buried her under that big gum tree across over there and they wasn't any Bible reading. Mrs. Yost never was right in her mind after that. I recollect her and Yost died a few years apart about the time of the Great War. They're buried out on the hill cemetery—but no one ever did move Nora."

I didn't hear any more. In a flash I remembered everything that had happened—the light that came soaring from the foot of the gum tree, the silky white mist Louise saw coming in the window and the little girl Blair saw walking barefoot in the cold. A cold sweat broke out all over me, my ears pounded—and I fainted.

Mother was rubbing my hands and holding camphor under my nose when I came to. I felt very weak. I think I never had been so ill before. I was afraid to go to bed. Mother pulled the old couch over by the fire and stayed with me through the night. Dorrie and Blair didn't go to the loft room either but curled up near the fire. I don't remember the old man being there. I suppose he went to bed in the haunted bedroom and probably slept all night. I must have dozed but it seemed ages before morning.

Father came home the next Friday as soon as the creeks were low enough to cross. He had found a place. When Mother told him Mr. Rice's story he was a little annoyed about the meddlesome old man but he could see how distressed we were.

"Pack your things," he said to Mother, looking at me compassionately. "I ain't putting you through no more. I'll take you all over to Ivy's tonight." Ivy was my mother's sister. "I'll get some fellows to help me move tomorrow."

And so we left the old Yost place. I didn't look back and I never went back—even to the neighborhood—until about 1962 and then only with companions.

The barn had burned down but the remnants of the house were still there. The gum tree stood, red as blood, in the bright October air in a thicket of green briars. We didn't linger. We drove on to the cemetery and looked at the old headstone of John Yost and his wife. On the way back we stopped at a fruit stand to buy some pears.

"They say that ridge is haunted," the farmer told me.

"People won't hardly go out there after dark." He inclined his head in the direction of my childhood home.

"How is it haunted?" I asked.

"I don't know. Fox hunters have shunned it for years. They say they see lights and things all along there."

I didn't press for more information. What could he add to what I already knew?